Christmas Plays
and
Biblical Skits

DRAMATIC ACTIVITIES FOR CHURCH GROUPS

BARBARA TENNEY

WESTBOW
PRESS®
A DIVISION OF THOMAS NELSON
& ZONDERVAN

WestBow Press books may be ordered through booksellers or by contacting:

WestBow Press
A Division of Thomas Nelson & Zondervan
1663 Liberty Drive
Bloomington, IN 47403
www.westbowpress.com
1 (866) 928-1240

ISBN: 978-1-5127-8395-7 (sc)
ISBN: 978-1-5127-8397-1 (hc)
ISBN: 978-1-5127-8396-4 (e)

Library of Congress Control Number: 2017906141

Print information available on the last page.

WestBow Press rev. date: 04/27/2017

To my father, Warren White, who died on Veteran's Day, November 11, 2016, at the age of ninety-five. He and Mom played Mary and Joseph in the Nativity at Burke Memorial United Methodist Church for many years.

Contents

Acknowledgments ix

Introduction xi

The Christmas Bazaar 1

Bernie "Don't Do" Christmas 11

A Joyful Noise 25

The Bus Trip 37

Flossie's No Bother 55

What's Missing? 77

Sonny Needs a Rest 98

Good Tidings of Great Joy 110

Biblical Skits

Jesus, Master of Metaphors 123

    1. The Wheat and the Tares 123

    2. The Mustard Seed 124

    3. The Wedding Garment 126

    4. Workers in the Vineyard 127

    5. Treasure in the Field 128

    6. Casting Net for Fish 129

    7. The Talents 130

    8. Forgiveness 131

The Prodigal Son 133

Interview with Simeon and Anna 136

Three Witnesses 139

Interview with Gideon 143

Where Is Your Treasure? 148

Back to "Normal" 152

Peter on Trial 156

Acknowledgments

A sincere thank-you to the following for their many contributions to this book and to my life.

- the Lord, who inspired me and gave me the words to write
- my loving husband, Garland, whose masterful computer skills were invaluable (Without him, this book never would have been compiled.)
- my family, who have always encouraged me
- my church family, who lovingly and patiently worked together to present the plays in our church (We had so much fun!)
- my youth class, Elijah and Adrianne, who were so willing to learn and bring the skits to life before the church
- faithful audiences who kept coming back to see the plays year after year

Introduction

In 2007, we were having trouble finding a Christmas play that would fit our situation. Our small church consisted mainly of adults and a few children. Financial resources were limited, so elaborate sets were out of the question. We used what we had or made what we needed.

God gave me the idea and words for *The Christmas Bazaar* while on a camping trip. The adults in the church performed the play that year.

After that, each summer someone would ask when I was going to go camping and write another play. So I did just that—I went camping and wrote another play. This continued for several years.

The cast fell in love with the characters, even Maudine, who insists on being in charge. Audiences wanted them back year after year. Maybe they saw themselves or someone they knew in one of these characters. As you get to know them, perhaps they will seem familiar to you, too.

Because we had so much fun with these plays, we offer them to you. Adapt the plays and skits to your own needs. Laugh and enjoy, yet celebrate the true meaning of Christmas.

I'd like to thank the wonderful, willing, eager, and encouraging cast at Burke Memorial Church. Thank you to the loving audiences who supported us over the years. First and foremost, I thank God, who made it all possible.

The Christmas Bazaar

Characters

Maudine. Elderly, take-charge type, always knows how things should be done
Harriet. Chairperson of the bazaar committee
Mavis. Committee member
Amelia. Committee member
Aunt Vera. Elderly, nearly deaf committee member
John. Volunteer
Stanley. Volunteer
Bill. Volunteer
Narrator
Mary
Joseph
Shepherds
Angels
Wise men

Setting. Meeting room at the church

Scene 1

Harriet, Mavis, and Amelia are seated at the table. Aunt Vera is rocking contentedly in a rocking chair. As they discuss plans, they keep looking nervously toward the door.

HARRIET, *looking at the to-do list.* Ladies, our Christmas church bazaar is just three weeks away. There are a few details we need to iron out this evening.

MAVIS. Like what?

HARRIET. Well, I've made a list of things we need to talk about. We can just go down through the list and make some decisions. Okay?

AUNT VERA. *Bouquet?* Am I supposed to bring a bouquet?

HARRIET. No, Aunt Vera, I said, "Okay."

AUNT VERA. Okay, I'll bring one.

AMELIA. Well, let's hurry up and get finished before *you-know-who* shows up. I do hope she doesn't bring one of her awful fruitcakes this year.

MAVIS. Yeah, I've never tasted anything like her fruitcake. You know we could have used her fruitcake in the foundation of the new fellowship hall.

AMELIA. I think we did! (*All giggle.*)

MAVIS. Is she really coming to the meeting?

HARRIET, *smiling mischievously.* I rather doubt it. I think for some reason she thinks the meeting starts at seven o'clock instead of six.

AMELIA. I wonder where she would have gotten that idea.

(*They all smile, very pleased with themselves.*)

HARRIET. First on the list is the menu for—

(*They are interrupted by the opening of the door as Maudine bursts into the room.*)

MAUDINE, *cheerfully.* Hel-lo! What are all of you doing here so early? I thought the meeting started at seven. It's a good thing I was passing by and saw the lights. I know how you value the benefit of my expert advice on these special occasions. Now that I'm here, we can get started. (*Pulls up a chair, sits down, and greets the women. Looks directly at Mavis.*) Mavis, dear, what happened to your hair?

MAVIS, *touching her hair.* What's wrong with my hair?

MAUDINE. Now don't worry about it, dear. It's nothing that can't be fixed. I'll have to give you the name of my hairdresser. She can do wonders. (*Pats Mavis's hand.*) Okay, what's first on the list?

HARRIET. We're discussing the menu. Now, some of the other ladies in the church will be bringing covered dishes.

MAVIS. I'll fix some chicken and dumplings.

AMELIA. I'm bringing a big tuna casserole. I got a new recipe from Betty.

AUNT VERA. Did somebody say *spaghetti*? Yeah, I'll make some spaghetti. You know I have a secret ingredient in my spaghetti sauce.

ALL IN UNISON. We know, Aunt Vera! *Oregano!*

AUNT VERA, *quietly with finger to lips.* Shh!

(*The others place their hands over their mouths.*)

MAUDINE. Of course, I'll bring my famous fruitcake. Everyone loves my fruitcake. Pastor Alvin would never forgive me if I didn't bring my famous fruitcake. He said he had never tasted anything like it! I don't know what Lucille does to hers. Maybe it's all that fruit she puts in it. Anyway, I'll bring six of my famous fruitcakes.

HARRIET. Oh, goody-goody! (*Boldly marks through first item on the list.*) Now, on to the next item on the agenda.

(*Door opens for two men with trash bags full of toys.*)

JOHN. Good evening, ladies. Where do you want us to put these bags of toys?

HARRIET. Oh, good! Just put them over there for now. Thank you, John. We're just starting to talk about the toy giveaway.

(*Bill enters with another filled trash bag.*)

BILL. Where do you want *this* one?

AMELIA. What's in that one?

BILL. I think it's full of candy. John, is that right?

AUNT VERA. *Bright!* You don't mean Andy Bright, do you? I don't know. I've heard stories about him. Somebody told me Andy and Preacher Alvin had a fallin' out over who won the bean toss game at Andy's frog fry. Of course, I wouldn't know if it's true or not—since *I* wasn't *invited*.

MAVIS. No, Aunt Vera. He wasn't talking about Andy. He was … Oh, never mind.

(*The men look at each and shrug the shoulders, confused—as the women thank them and begin examining the toy bags.*)

AMELIA. These are beautiful toys we're giving away. People have been so generous. These will make a lot of children very happy this Christmas.

HARRIET. Yes, it looks like we'll have an abundance of goods!

AUNT VERA. *Hoods?* Hubie Hoods? Oh, I just love that man!

MAUDINE. I don't know about *giving* these toys away.

AMELIA. What do you mean, Maudine? That's why we gathered them up, to give away.

MAUDINE. They're too good to just give away. We'll sell them! The church could always use the money. After all, we do have the Ladies Circle trip to Charleston coming up in the spring. Yes, that's what we'll do. We'll sell them!

(*The women lay the toys down, look at each other, sigh, and retake their seats at the table.*)

HARRIET, *boldly marking second item off list.* Next item. Who's in charge of the clothing giveaway?

MAVIS. Sylvia volunteered to do that, but she couldn't be at the meeting today. She's looking forward to seeing the happy faces of the people when they come in to pick out clothing for their families.

MAUDINE. You don't mean they are actually coming inside the church—wet and all—on the new carpet?

AMELIA. Maudine, how will they get their clothing if they don't come in?

MAUDINE. Well now, listen to this idea. I was thinking maybe we could be like MacRonald's and have a "drive-by-and-pick-up" window! It would save the new carpet from getting wet and muddy.

(*All except Maudine roll their eyes upward.*)

HARRIET, *boldly marking through another item as they all look at each other.* Okay, about the fruit baskets. Do they have them ready to be given out to the shut-ins?

MAVIS. Yes, I think they're about to finish.

AUNT VERA. What's that about spinach? Never did care much for spinach myself.

MAVIS. No, Aunt Vera, not spinach—finish. They're about to finish. Oh, never mind.

HARRIET. I think it would be nice to deliver the fruit baskets on Christmas Eve.

MAUDINE. Harriet, I'll help you check the records for this year.

HARRIET. What kind of records? Why do we need to check any records?

MAUDINE. Well, I think we should only give fruit baskets to the shut-ins who have attended at least half the services this year.

HARRIET, *vigorously marking through item on list. All are getting weary.* Last on our agenda is the matter of providing refreshments to the carolers.

MAVIS. We were thinking about serving cookies and hot chocolate.

MAUDINE. That sounds good. A dollar for the cookies, and a dollar for the hot chocolate. I'll make cookies. They'll gladly pay a dollar for *my* cookies.

HARRIET, That does it! (*Emphatically lays down pencil, stands up to leave.*) I need to get a drink of water.

MAVIS, *standing up.* I need to get something to eat.

AMELIA, *standing up.* I need to ... there has to be *something* I need to do.

(*They get Aunt Vera and start to leave.*)

MAUDINE. You girls go ahead. I'm going to sit here and rest awhile. All this planning has made me tired. It sounds like the church is going to make a lot of money this Christmas. (*She goes to rocking chair.*)

HARRIET, *speaking to the others at door, looking back at Maudine.* Poor Maudine. She has no idea what Christmas is all about. (*They exit.*)

(*Maudine falls asleep in the chair. Curtain closes.*)

Scene 2

The Nativity

(*Curtain opens with Joseph, Mary, and baby Jesus on center stage. Narrator reads all scripture from offstage.*)

NARRATOR, *reading Luke 2:1–7.* And it came to pass in those days, that there went out a decree from Caesar Augustus, that all the world should be taxed. (And this taxing was first made when Cyrenius was governor of Syria.) And all went to be taxed, every one into his own city. And Joseph also went up from Galilee, out of the city of Nazareth, into Judaea, unto the city of David, which is called Bethlehem; (because he was of the house and lineage of David:) To be taxed with Mary his espoused wife, being great with child. And so it was, that, while they were there, the days were accomplished that she should be delivered. And she brought forth her firstborn son, and wrapped him in swaddling clothes, and laid him in a manger; because there was no room for them in the inn.

("What Child Is This?" is played or sung.)

NARRATOR, *reading Luke 2:8.* And there were in the same country shepherds abiding in the field, keeping watch over their flock by night.

(Shepherds walk up aisle toward stage; they huddle at front, stage right)

NARRATOR, *reading Luke 2:9–12.* And, lo, the angel of the Lord came upon them, and the glory of the Lord shone round about them: and they were sore afraid. And the angel said unto them, Fear not: for, behold, I bring you good tidings of great joy, which shall be to all people. For unto you is born this day in the city of David a Saviour, which is Christ the Lord. And this shall be a sign unto you; Ye shall find the babe wrapped in swaddling clothes, lying in a manger.

(An angel appears to the shepherds, who are frightened.)

NARRATOR, *reading Luke 2:13–14.* And suddenly there was with the angel a multitude of the heavenly host praising God, and saying, Glory to God in the highest, and on earth peace, good will toward men.

(A multitude of angels join first angel.)

NARRATOR, *reading Luke 2:15.* And it came to pass, as the angels were gone away from them into heaven, the shepherds said one to another, Let us now go even unto Bethlehem, and see this thing which is come to pass, which the Lord hath made known unto us.

(Angels stand behind Mary, Joseph, and Jesus at back center stage.)

NARRATOR, *reading Luke 2:16.* And they came with haste, and found Mary, and Joseph, and the babe lying in a manger.

(Shepherds quickly enter stage right, beside the manger.)

NARRATOR, *reading Matthew 2:1–2.* Now when Jesus was born in Bethlehem of Judaea in the days of Herod the king, behold, there came wise men from the east to Jerusalem, Saying, Where is he that is born King of the Jews? for we have seen his star in the east, and are come to worship him.

(As song "We Three Kings" is played, the wise men come slowly up aisle toward stage, stopping at stage left, beside the manger. Each carries a gift.)

NARRATOR, *reading Matthew 2:11.* And when they were come into the house, they saw the young child with Mary his mother, and fell down, and worshipped him: and when they had opened their treasures, they presented unto him gifts; gold, and frankincense, and myrrh.

(Wise men kneel one at a time, present gifts to Jesus, and then stand.)

NARRATOR, *reading John 3:16–17.* For God so loved the world, that he gave his only begotten Son, that whosoever believeth on him should not perish, but have everlasting life. For God sent not his Son into the world to condemn the world; but that the world through him might be saved.

("O Holy Night" is sung as solo. Curtain closes.)

Scene 3

(Curtain opens with Maudine still asleep in the chair.)

MAUDINE, *speaking to herself as she awakens.* I just had the most wonderful dream! I dreamed I held baby Jesus in my arms. *(Picks up baby doll.)* I was a little girl again, and the doll I was holding was the baby Jesus. (*Cradles the doll and sings one verse of "Away in a Manger."*)

(*The other women return as Maudine is singing and look at her with puzzled expressions.*)

MAUDINE, *taking baby doll to show the women.* Look, girls, isn't it beautiful? Just like baby Jesus! I've just seen what Christmas is really about. It's not about things or money; it's about people. It's about loving and caring for each other, about giving of ourselves without expecting anything in return. It's about Jesus and the joy he brings to your heart.

Well, girls, why are we standing around? We have things to do! Those little boys and girls are not going to get these toys with us just standing around. We have to spread some Christmas cheer. After all, isn't that what Christmas is really about?

(*They all hug and wish each other, "Merry Christmas."*)

(*Curtain closes as they busy themselves with toys*)

End

Bernie "Don't Do" Christmas

Characters

Aunt Vera: Elderly woman, nearly deaf
Harriet: Attends Aunt Vera
Bernie: Aunt Vera's younger brother
Violet: Bernie's wife
Maudine: Elderly, take-charge type
Richard: Maudine's husband
Mavis
Lydia: Mavis's sister
Amelia
John: Amelia's husband
Pastor Smith
Mrs. Smith: Pastor's wife
Narrator
Mary
Joseph
Shepherds
Angels
Wise men

Setting: Christmas Eve at Aunt Vera's home

Scene 1

(*Everyone gathers at Aunt Vera's house for preprogram dinner. As guests arrive, each places a covered dish on the table and a gift under the tree for Aunt Vera.*)

AUNT VERA, *rising from her chair. She goes to window, looks out in anticipation.* I figured they'd here by now.

HARRIET, *sitting quietly and knitting, notices Aunt Vera wandering around.* Now, Aunt Vera, come sit down. It's still early. Everybody will be here soon. We'll have plenty of time to eat and then go to the church for the Christmas program later.

AUNT VERA. Waiter? We don't need a waiter! I figured everybody could help themselves to the food and not have to be served.

HARRIET. No, Aunt Vera, I didn't say "waiter." I said … Never mind. You're right. We all can serve ourselves. (*Helps Aunt Vera to chair.*)

AUNT VERA. I can't wait to see my little brother Bernie! That's what I like about Christmas. It's a time to get together with family and friends—even though Bernie "don't do" Christmas.

HARRIET, *stunned.* What do you mean, he "don't do" Christmas?

AUNT VERA. Oh, Bernie used to celebrate Christmas in a big way. He used to buy gifts for all the neighborhood children and made sure nobody went hungry on Christmas. Why, he was a shepherd in the church Nativity scene for years. (*She chuckles.*) I still remember the time he tripped over Pastor Alvin's robe, and they both fell into Margaret Kittle's lap. She was always a shepherd, too. They like to never got them all untangled. (*Rises and looks out window.*) But then, he bought that store, and it takes up about all his time. I don't see him much anymore.

HARRIET. Well, they should be here soon. Come on over here, and sit down in your chair.

AUNT VERA. My hair? Do I need to comb my hair?

HARRIET, *smiling.* No, Aunt Vera, your hair is fine.

(*Aunt Vera sits. Action on stage freezes. Bernie and Violet enter and start up the aisle. He carries a small bag, She carries a gift for Aunt Vera.*)

VIOLET, *sarcastically.* I do hope you don't dislocate your shoulder carrying all that food you brought for dinner.

BERNIE. Just never you mind. With what everyone else brings, I'm sure this will be enough. Besides, you know me. I don't like to be a show-off.

VIOLET. Yeah, Bernie. After all these years, I know you.

BERNIE, *arriving at door.* I hope Vera can hear the doorbell. (*As he rings, a loud bell sounds. Violet and Bernie look around, as if wondering where such a loud sound came from.*)

AUNT VERA. That must be my Bernie! (*Excitedly goes to door and opens it.*) Oh, Bernie and Violet, I'm so glad to see you! Come in! Come in! (*Hugs them.*) Harriet, this is my baby brother, Bernie, and his wife, Violet. Bernie, this is Harriet, my very dear friend.

HARRIET. I'm very glad to meet you. Aunt Vera has told me a lot about you. Here, let me help you with this. (*Reaches into the bag Bernie's carrying and takes out one loaf of bread; looks curiously at Bernie.*)

BERNIE. I didn't want to be a show-off.

HARRIET. Oh, okay. (*Places bread on table.*) Aunt Vera had me fix the guest room for you to spend the night.

AUNT VERA, *emphatically*. Light, yes. We do need more light! Hundred-watt bulbs! That's what we need!

(*They all turn and look at Aunt Vera.*)

BERNIE. No, we can't spend the night. We just came to eat supper with Vera. I have to be at the store early in the morning.

HARRIET. But tomorrow's Christmas!

BERNIE. That's right. There will be lots of last-minute shoppers looking for bargains. I've got Sam working, but I'll have to go in to make sure everything goes all right.

VIOLET. I tried to tell him that Sam would like to be home with his family for Christmas.

BERNIE. I've got that covered. I gave him a coupon for five dollars off a ham or turkey at Smallmart. And I told him he wouldn't have to stay all day—he could leave at five instead of six. (*Action on stage freezes.*)

(*Maudine enters and starts up the aisle.*)

MAUDINE. *noticing Richard is not there.* Come on, Richard. We don't want to be late. After all, I am the director. How would it look for the director to be late? I pride myself on not being late to these social functions. I'll not have you making us late!

RICHARD. Yes, dear. (*Enters with arms loaded with packages and starts toward Maudine*) It just took me a while to get everything out of the car.

MAUDINE. Well, here, dear, let me help you. (*Takes a small package.*) Now hurry up, Richard.

RICHARD. Hurrying up, dear.

(*Arriving at the door, they ring the bell and look around, wondering where the loud bell sound came from.*)

AUNT VERA, *going to door.* Why, it's Maudine and Richard. Do come in. (*Hugs them.*) Good to see you, Richard. I was afraid you wouldn't be able to come.

RICHARD. I was able to get all my chores done.

MAUDINE. Now, Richard, I told you that you didn't have to do everything. You could leave the vacuuming and dusting until after the program.

RICHARD. Yes, dear, but after the program I have to do the kitchen and bathroom.

MAUDINE. Oh! That's right!

AUNT VERA. I want you to meet my brother, Bernie, and his wife, Violet. They're going to eat supper with us.

MAUDINE. Well, that's nice.

AUNT VERA. Rice? I guess if someone brings some, then we'll have rice. Don't care much for rice myself. (*Shivers.*)

MAUDINE, *to Harriet.* Are they going to the Christmas program after supper?

HARRIET. Oh, no. Bernie "don't do" Christmas.

MAUDINE. What do you mean, he "don't do" Christmas? (*Action on stage freezes.*)

(*Mavis and Lydia enter and start up the aisle.*)

MAVIS. Are you feeling better now?

LYDIA, *whining.* A little bit. My stomach has finally left the roller coaster, I think.

MAVIS. Well, it was very embarrassing, you hanging your head out the window like a dog.

LYDIA. I couldn't help it. You were driving too fast.

MAVIS. I was only doing twenty-five miles per hour.

LYDIA. That's what I mean. I couldn't take it!

MAVIS. Well, we're here now. You'll be okay.

(*They ring the bell and look around as if to see where the sound came from.*)

AUNT VERA, *opening door.* Come in, girls. Supper's almost ready.

LYDIA. Oh, good. I'm starving!

(*Mavis gives Lydia a disbelieving look as Aunt Vera introduces Mavis and Lydia to the others.*)

MAVIS. Hello, Maudine. Isn't that the same dress you wore last year?

MAUDINE. Well! Certainly not! It's the same colors! That's it! It's the same colors!

Mavis, *to Maudine.* It's nice that Bernie and his wife will be here to celebrate Christmas with Aunt Vera.

Maudine. Haven't you heard? Bernie "don't do" Christmas.

Lydia. (*to Mavis*) That *is* the same dress she wore last year!

Mavis, *ignoring Lydia's comment.* What do you mean, he "don't do" Christmas?

(*Action on stage freezes, as John and Amelia start up the aisle.*)

Amelia, *carrying her angel costume.* John, I don't think my costume was really too long, do you?

John. Huh-uh.

Amelia. But I guess if Maudine said to fix it, then I'd better fix it. After all, she is the director. Right?

John. Uh-huh.

Amelia. We're not late, are we?

John. Huh-uh.

Amelia. Did you get Aunt Vera's gift?

John. Uh-huh.

(*arrive at the door, ring bell and look around wondering where the loud sound came from.*)

Aunt Vera, *opening door.* Oh, sakes alive! Look who's here. It's Amelia and Johnny. Hello, Amelia. John, are you doing okay?

JOHN. Uh-huh.

AUNT VERA. Come on in. I want you to meet my brother, Bernie, and Violet, his wife.

AMELIA. Glad to meet you folks. I didn't even know Aunt Vera had a brother.

AUNT VERA. Mother? Yes, he's the spitting image of our mother, except she wore her hair a little bit longer.

AMELIA. Maudine, do you think this will be okay? (*Shows Maudine the costume.*)

MAUDINE. Why, yes, dear, that's fine. Even though I *am* the director, I've never been the type of person to order people around.

MAVIS, *approaches Amelia and whispers.* Bernie "don't do" Christmas.

AMELIA, *gasps and turns to John.* Bernie "don't do" Christmas!

HARRIET. We'd better start eating. It'll be time to go to the program soon. Aunt Vera, would you say grace? (*Everyone bows head.*)

(*Curtain closes.*)

SCENE 2

(*Aunt Vera's house after supper. Some are cleaning up the table while others are seated, resting after the big meal.*)

AUNT VERA. I don't know when I've eaten so much good food. I may have to call Weight Watchers.

MAUDINE. Richard, I do hope your costume will still fit you.

RICHARD. Well, if yours fits you, mine should be all right.

(*Knock on back door. Everyone is reluctant to get up to see who it is.*)

HARRIET. Oh, I'll get it. (*Gets up and opens door.*) Hello, Pastor. Do come in. (*to others*) It's Pastor and Mrs. Smith. You're a little late for supper, but I'm sure we can still find something for you to eat.

PASTOR. Thanks, Harriet. We've already eaten. But I'm glad you're all still here. We've just come from Charlie's house. He's not feeling very well and won't be able to come to the program.

MRS. SMITH. That poor family has had such a rough time lately.

BERNIE. What's wrong with Charlie?

MAVIS. His little girl, Sally, is very sick. The doctors say that she'll be all right, but it's going to take a long time. They have to stay up with her most nights. They're pretty much worn out.

AMELIA. They have lots of bills to pay, and with Charlie losing his job at the sawmill, they don't know how they're gonna pay them.

MRS. SMITH. It doesn't look like they will have much of a Christmas. They won't be able to buy any gifts for the children.

RICHARD. I wish there was something we could do to help them.

MAUDINE, *suddenly getting an idea.* Say! I'm fixing a huge ham for Christmas dinner. No way Richard and I can eat it all. I'll take some to Charlie and his family.

AMELIA. And I love to cook. I can make some extra pies.

AUNT VERA. Did somebody say "fries"? I like fries, but right now I don't think I could hold another bite.

LYDIA. I have some extra gifts I can wrap up for the kids.

RICHARD. John, maybe you and I could cut some firewood for them and help out with some of the chores. Can we do that?

JOHN. Uh-huh.

BERNIE, *speaking quietly to Pastor.* Are these people really going to spend their time and money helping out somebody else instead of being home with their own families on Christmas?

PASTOR. That's the way they are! They realize what Jesus meant when he said, "It's more blessed to give than to receive," especially at Christmas.

MAVIS. Hey, everybody. I just remembered. Charlie was supposed to be a shepherd. Who's going to take his place?

HARRIET. Bernie, why don't you take Charlie's place? Somebody told me that you've been a shepherd before.

BERNIE, *hesitating.* I don't know.

EVERYONE. Oh, please, Bernie. We need you!

BERNIE, *reluctantly.* Well, okay, if you think I can.

PASTOR. Thanks, Bernie. Let's go, everybody. We have things to do and a program to put on!

(*Curtain closes.*)

SCENE 3

The Nativity

(Curtain opens with Joseph, Mary, and baby Jesus on center stage. Narrator reads all scripture from offstage.)

NARRATOR, *reading Luke 2:1–7.* And it came to pass in those days, that there went out a decree from Caesar Augustus, that all the world should be taxed. (And this taxing was first made when Cyrenius was governor of Syria.) And all went to be taxed, every one into his own city. And Joseph also went up from Galilee, out of the city of Nazareth, into Judaea, unto the city of David, which is called Bethlehem; (because he was of the house and lineage of David:) To be taxed with Mary his espoused wife, being great with child. And so it was, that, while they were there, the days were accomplished that she should be delivered. And she brought forth her firstborn son, and wrapped him in swaddling clothes, and laid him in a manger; because there was no room for them in the inn.

("What Child Is This?" is played or sung,)

NARRATOR, *reading Luke 2:8.* And there were in the same country shepherds abiding in the field, keeping watch over their flock by night.

(Shepherds walk up aisle toward stage; they huddle at front, just off stage right.)

NARRATOR, *reading Luke 2:9–12.* And, lo, the angel of the Lord came upon them, and the glory of the Lord shone round about them: and they were sore afraid. And the angel said unto them, Fear not: for, behold, I bring you good tidings of great joy, which shall be to all people. For unto you is born this day in the city of David a Saviour,

which is Christ the Lord. And this shall be a sign unto you; Ye shall find the babe wrapped in swaddling clothes, lying in a manger.

(*An angel appears to the shepherds, who are frightened.*)

NARRATOR, *reading Luke 2:13–14.* And suddenly there was with the angel a multitude of the heavenly host praising God, and saying, Glory to God in the highest, and on earth peace, good will toward men.

(*A multitude of angels join first angel.*)

NARRATOR, *reading Luke 2:15.* And it came to pass, as the angels were gone away from them into heaven, the shepherds said one to another, Let us now go even unto Bethlehem, and see this thing which is come to pass, which the Lord hath made known unto us.

(*Angels stand behind Mary, Joseph, and Jesus at back center stage.*)

NARRATOR, *reading Luke 2:16.* And they came with haste, and found Mary, and Joseph, and the babe lying in a manger.

(*Shepherds quickly enter stage right, beside the manger.*)

NARRATOR, *reading Matthew 2:1–2.* Now when Jesus was born in Bethlehem of Judaea in the days of Herod the king, behold, there came wise men from the east to Jerusalem, Saying, Where is he that is born King of the Jews? for we have seen his star in the east, and are come to worship him.

(*As song "We Three Kings" is played, the wise men come slowly up aisle toward stage, stopping at stage left, beside manger. Each carries a gift.*)

NARRATOR, *reading Matthew 2:11.* And when they were come into the house, they saw the young child with Mary his mother, and fell down, and worshipped him: and when they had opened their treasures, they presented unto him gifts; gold, and frankincense, and myrrh.

(*Wise men kneel one at a time, present gifts to Jesus, and then stand.*)

NARRATOR, *reading John 3:16–17.* For God so loved the world, that he gave his only begotten Son, that whosoever believeth on him should not perish, but have everlasting life. For God sent not his Son into the world to condemn the world; but that the world through him might be saved.

(*"O Holy Night" is sung as solo. During song, Bernie steps from his place as shepherd and kneels before the manger. Everyone except Bernie looks at each other and smiles.*)

(*Curtain closes.*)

SCENE 4

(*Aunt Vera and Harriet are alone at Vera's house after the program.*)

HARRIET. I think that was the best Nativity scene we've ever had.

AUNT VERA. I do too! It did my heart good to see Bernie as a shepherd again, and when he knelt down, I could have shouted. By the way, where did Bernie and Violet go?

HARRIET. He said they would be along. He had some calls to make. (*Door opens.*) I bet that's them now. (*Bernie and Violet enter.*)

BERNIE. Vera, do you still have that spare room ready for us? It looks like we *will* be spending the night and Christmas Day. I called some friends of mine. The bank is going to set up a fund to help Charlie pay his bills. Dr. Jones at the clinic thinks he can arrange some free medical help for little Sally. And, another thing, we've been very busy at the store lately. I think we could use an extra hand. Sam and Charlie would get along fine together. Speaking of Sam, I called and told him to lock up the store until after Christmas and to take home a big ham. (*Laughs.*) He couldn't believe it was me—kept asking for further identification.

AUNT VERA. I've been praying for you, Bernie, all these years.

BERNIE. I know you have, Vera. I'm glad you didn't stop.

AUNT VERA. Pop? Why, sure, Bernie, there's some cold pop in the kitchen. Help yourself.

(*Bernie laughs.*)

VIOLET, *to Harriet.* I've been waiting a long time to see Bernie "do" Christmas again!

(*Curtain closes.*)

End

A Joyful Noise

Characters

Jim: Church janitor
Aunt Vera: Elderly lady, nearly deaf
Harriet: Choir director
Bernie: Aunt Vera's younger brother
Violet: Bernie's Wife
Maudine: Elderly, take-charge type
Richard: Maudine's husband
Mavis
Lydia: Mavis's sister
Amelia
John: Amelia's husband
Olive: New choir member
Annabelle: Choir member

Scene 1

Setting: Church choir room, with chairs set up.

(*Curtain opens as janitor Jim busily sweeps up before the choir arrives.*)

JIM, *to audience.* Good evening to all of you and a very Merry Christmas! I'm the janitor here at this little church. Have been for nigh on fifty years. They call me Jim. I do the sweepin', moppin', dustin'... most anything that needs to be done. (*Chuckles.*) Now and then they even have me workin' on the furnace or air conditionin'—if you can believe that.

This is my favorite time of year—Christmas. The birthday of our Lord and Savior, Jesus Christ. It's a happy time. A time when folks are kind and helpful to one another, spreadin' joy and good cheer all around. Speaking of spreadin' joy, the choir is gonna be here soon to start practicin' for this year's program. They'll be makin' that joyful noise that David talked about in the book of Psalms. If you listen close you might even hear that hallelujah ring in it. I think I hear them comin' now!

(*Maudine and Richard enter from back room. Richard stops to greet Jim as Maudine proceeds across stage, obviously thrilled with being there. Jim continues sweeping on stage right.*)

MAUDINE. Richard, I can hardly control myself! I'm so excited! Just think! In a little while, this hall will be reverberating again with tones of celestial quality—my voice! I could almost cry!

RICHARD, *looking at Jim.* Yeah, me too. (*Gets choir books.*) It looks like we're the first ones here. I could have finished my nap. (*Hands book to Maudine.*)

JIM. Oh, Richard, I wanted to tell you … I think you did a fine job leading the service last Sunday.

RICHARD. Well, thank you, Jim! I appreciate the kind words.

MAUDINE. Come on, Richard. Sit down.

RICHARD. Yes, dear.

(*Jim continues sweeping.*)

MAVIS, *entering from back room with Lydia.* If I hear you sing that song one more time, I'm gonna scream!

LYDIA, *following Mavis.* I'm just practicing! I thought I might get to sing a solo part this year.

MAVIS, *sweetly.* I hope you *do* get to sing a solo this year. (*Lydia looks surprised and happy.*) So low I can't hear it!

(*Lydia frowns and mumbles to herself.*)

JIM. The Bible says to make a joyful noise unto the Lord.

MAVIS. I don't know about the joyful part, but she has the noise part down pat. (*Mavis and Lydia greet Maudine and Richard, pick up their books, and sit down.*)

OLIVE, *entering quickly.* Oh, Lydia, may I sit next to you? I'm glad you asked me to join the choir, but I'm kinda nervous.

LYDIA. Sure. Come right over here. I might get to sing a solo this year, you know.

OLIVE. Oh, really? That would be great!

(*Amelia and John enter from back room.*)

RICHARD. Here comes John and Amelia. Hey, John, doing okay?

JOHN. Uh- huh!

AMELIA, *picking up books.* Hi, everyone! Are we ready to sing?

MAUDINE. Amelia, dear, I'm rather surprised to see you here. Someone said you weren't singing in the choir this year.

AMELIA. Maudine, why wouldn't I sing in the choir? I love to sing.

MAUDINE. I think it was something about your not being able to hit those high notes last year.

AMELIA. You tell that *someone* that I'm doing better. I stand on my tip-toes! Don't I, John?

JOHN. Uh-huh.

JIM. John, would you like to go with me on Friday to take some gifts to the nursing home down the road?

JOHN. Uh-huh.

JIM. Good! They look forward to us coming every year. I'll pick you up at six. (*Hums as he continues to work.*)

(*Aunt Vera, Harriet, Bernie, and Violet enter from back room. Jim notices Aunt Vera.*)

JIM. Well, bless my soul! Look who's here! How are you, Miss Vera?

AUNT VERA. I'm just fine, Jim. And how are you doing?

JIM. Doin' real good, Miss Vera. The Lord's blessin' me every day! Are you gonna sing in the choir?

AUNT VERA. Huh? What's that you say?

JIM, *speaking louder.* I say, are you singin' in the choir?

AUNT VERA. Oh, yeah, yeah, been sittin' by the fire.

BERNIE. We were coming to practice, and Vera wanted to come along and listen.

HARRIET. (*pointing to chair*) Sit down here, Aunt Vera. This should be comfortable for you.

AUNT VERA. Thank you, dear. (*Chuckles.*) You know, I can't carry a tune in a bucket—but I do have two good ears!

HARRIET, *starting toward music stand.* We're thrilled to have Bernie and Violet in the choir this year. They'll help to give it more of a rich, full-bodied sound.

VIOLET. I'm afraid when *we* start singing, everybody will wish they had two good ears like Vera.

HARRIET. I'm sure it will sound fine. Okay, if everybody's ready we'll try page twenty-one first, "Joy to the World."

(*Annabelle enters from back room.*)

ANNABELLE. I'm so sorry I'm late. Maudine, didn't you say you were going to pick me up on the way here?

MAUDINE, *suddenly remembering.* Oh! (*Turns to Richard.*) Richard, you forgot to pick up Annabelle! Really, dear, do try to be more responsible!

RICHARD. Yes, dear. I'll try.

JIM. Well, I'd love to stay and listen, but I'd better see what's wrong with the furnace. It's been singin' out of tune lately. (*Waves to choir.*) I'll be back later. (*Stops by Aunt Vera's chair.*) Merry Christmas, Miss Vera, and God bless you.

AUNT VERA. God bless you, Jimmy.

(*Harriet directs choir to rise. Maudine goes to piano and begins playing at Harriet's signal. Maudine plays intro, missing notes now and then. Everyone frowns.*)

HARRIET, *turning book over, looking at the pages.* Page twenty-one, Maudine.

MAUDINE. Yes, dear, that's what I have. Is there a problem?

(*Everyone except Maudine looks at each other.*)

HARRIET. Okay, let's try it again.

(*Maudine plays intro again making mistakes. Choir begins singing softly, unsure of themselves.*)

HARRIET, *stopping choir.* Oh, come on now. We can do better than that. Put some feeling into it. Maudine, give us a note.

(*Maudine sings out a loud, shrill sound. Startled, everyone looks at Maudine. Aunt Vera comes forward in her chair, looking for the source of the sound.*)

HARRIET. On the piano, Maudine! Give us a note on the piano.

MAUDINE. Oh, okay! (*Plays a note on the piano; everyone starts singing, except Amelia.*)

HARRIET. What's wrong, Amelia?

AMELIA. Maudine made me lose my pitch!

(*Everyone but Maudine and Harriet nods in agreement.*)

AUNT VERA. Can you sing "Silent Night"? It's my favorite.

RICHARD. Well, I know we can do *that* one.

HARRIET. Page five. Aunt Vera, this is for you.

(*They begin singing; someone starts singing noticeably late.*)

MAVIS. Somebody's coming in late.

LYDIA. It was John.

JOHN. Huh-uh!

AMELIA. I think it was Violet.

VIOLET. I was just following *you*.

AUNT VERA. Oh, yes! Sounds good. "Silent Night" was always my favorite.

LYDIA, *raising her hand*. I'd be glad to do a solo part this year. Mavis can tell you I've been practicing.

MAVIS. Has she ever!

HARRIET. I haven't really decided on the solo parts yet, but I had thought about John. John, would you do a solo part?

JOHN. *Huh-uh!*

HARRIET. Okay, never mind. We'll decide the solo parts later. Let's see how we can do with page ten. (*Gives Maudine a sign and lifts arms to direct.*)

AMELIA, *interrupting*. I don't know this one.

BERNIE. I don't either. Never heard it before.

HARRIET. That's why we're practicing—to learn it.

LYDIA. Maybe we should practice in the mornings. I sing better in the morning.

RICHARD. Yeah, I'm getting hoarse.

MAUDINE. Richard, I'll not have you getting hoarse during choir practice.

RICHARD. Yes, dear. I must have been mistaken.

HARRIET, *closing book; throwing up hands.* Everybody take a break. (*Sits down and shakes her head.*)

AUNT VERA. Cake? That sounds good. All this good singing has made me hungry. (*Turns to Harriet.*) What's wrong, child?

HARRIET. Don't ask! Nothing's going right. We haven't gotten through even one song. Something is definitely missing.

AUNT VERA. Sounds to me like it's time to pray. Hey, everybody! Let's … (*Sees no one is paying attention, so she whistles loudly and folds hands to pray. Everyone bows head in prayer.*) Dear Lord, we all need your help again. Harriet says something is missing from the singing. As we practice, please send us what we need, so we can make a joyful noise unto you. Thanks for listening, Lord. I'll talk to you again later tonight.

(*Everyone on stage freezes in position. Curtain closes. Stage is set for Nativity behind curtain*)

JIM, *speaking to audience in front of curtain at stage right.* It's been a long time since Jesus, our Savior, came to earth. He was a heavenly king, yet he chose to come to earth as a baby and was placed in a lowly manger. Let's go back to Bethlehem and experience the joy of that first Christmas morn. (*Steps behind curtain.*)

Scene 2

The Nativity

(Curtain opens with Joseph, Mary, and baby Jesus on center stage. Narrator reads all scripture from offstage.)

NARRATOR, *reading Luke 2:1–7.* And it came to pass in those days, that there went out a decree from Caesar Augustus, that all the world should be taxed. (And this taxing was first made when Cyrenius was governor of Syria.) And all went to be taxed, every one into his own city. And Joseph also went up from Galilee, out of the city of Nazareth, into Judaea, unto the city of David, which is called Bethlehem; (because he was of the house and lineage of David:) To be taxed with Mary his espoused wife, being great with child. And so it was, that, while they were there, the days were accomplished that she should be delivered. And she brought forth her firstborn son, and wrapped him in swaddling clothes, and laid him in a manger; because there was no room for them in the inn.

("What Child Is This?" is played or sung.)

NARRATOR, *reading Luke 2:8.* And there were in the same country shepherds abiding in the field, keeping watch over their flock by night.

(Shepherds walk up aisle toward stage; they huddle at front, just off stage right.)

NARRATOR, *reading Luke 2:9–12.* And, lo, the angel of the Lord came upon them, and the glory of the Lord shone round about them: and they were sore afraid. And the angel said unto them, Fear not: for, behold, I bring you good tidings of great joy, which shall be to all people. For unto you is born this day in the city of David a Saviour,

which is Christ the Lord. And this shall be a sign unto you; Ye shall find the babe wrapped in swaddling clothes, lying in a manger.

(*An angel appears to the shepherds, who are frightened.*)

Narrator, *reading Luke 2:13–14.* And suddenly there was with the angel a multitude of the heavenly host praising God, and saying, Glory to God in the highest, and on earth peace, good will toward men.

(*A multitude of angels join first angel.*)

Narrator, *reading Luke 2:15.* And it came to pass, as the angels were gone away from them into heaven, the shepherds said one to another, Let us now go even unto Bethlehem, and see this thing which is come to pass, which the Lord hath made known unto us.

(*Angels stand behind Mary, Joseph, and Jesus at back center stage.*)

Narrator, *reading Luke 2:16.* And they came with haste, and found Mary, and Joseph, and the babe lying in a manger.

(*Shepherds quickly enter stage right, beside the manger.*)

Narrator, *reading Matthew 2:1–2.* Now when Jesus was born in Bethlehem of Judaea in the days of Herod the king, behold, there came wise men from the east to Jerusalem, Saying, Where is he that is born King of the Jews? for we have seen his star in the east, and are come to worship him.

As song "We Three Kings" is played, the wise men come slowly up aisle toward stage, stopping at stage left, beside the manger. Each carries a gift.)

Narrator, *reading Matthew 2:11.* And when they were come into the house, they saw the young child with Mary his mother, and fell down, and worshipped him: and when they had opened their treasures, they presented unto him gifts; gold, and frankincense, and myrrh.

(*Wise men kneel one at a time, present gifts to Jesus, and then stand.*)

NARRATOR, *reading John 3:16–17.* For God so loved the world, that he gave his only begotten Son, that whosoever believeth on him should not perish, but have everlasting life. For God sent not his Son into the world to condemn the world; but that the world through him might be saved.

(*"O Holy Night" is sung as solo. Curtain closes.*)

Scene 3

(*Curtain opens with choir members on stage in same positions as end of scene 1.*)

HARRIET. Thank you, Aunt Vera, for that wonderful prayer. Now (*to choir*), let's see what we can do with page two.

(*Harriet lifts arms to direct. Choir messes up. Harriet stops them. A voice continues singing offstage. They all go to back door. Jim enters, singing and sweeping, oblivious to the attention. All are amazed by his voice.*)

ANNABELLE. Jim! We didn't know you could sing like that!

JIM. Oh, I don't do anything special. I just try to make a joyful noise, especially this time of year.

HARRIET. Why haven't you been singing in the choir?

JIM. I never really thought about it. Nobody ever asked me.

BERNIE. Well, we're asking you now. I think we all agree that we need you.

VIOLET. Now I think we know what's been missing—you and your Christmas spirit!

AMELIA. Yeah, the *joy* is what's been missing all along.

AUNT VERA. I think God has just answered our prayer. Jim has the Christmas joy all year round. He's always giving to help others. We can make a noise, but we need the Christmas spirit to make a *joyful* noise unto the Lord.

RICHARD. Jim, you have shown us that we need to have joy in our *hearts* before we can have it in our song.

MAUDINE, *taking Richard's arm with pride.* Oh, Richard, how sweet.

RICHARD, *patting Maudine's hand.* Thank you, dear.

HARRIET. Okay, let's try again. And this time I want to hear that *joy* in your song!

AUNT VERA. *Sing along?* Yes, I think I *will* sing along! Come on, Jimmy, let's sing! (Jim joins in.)

(*Choir sings joyfully one verse of "Joy to the World"*)

End

The Bus Trip

Characters

Bus Driver
Aunt Vera: Elderly lady, nearly deaf
Harriet
Granddad Miller
Grandma Miller
Sarah: Granddaughter, age 8-10
Maudine
Richard: Maudine's husband
Mavis
Lydia: Mavis's sister
Amelia
John: Amelia's husband
Annabelle
Pastor Smith
Narrator
Mary
Joseph
Shepherds
Angels
Wise men

Scene 1

Setting: a humble country cottage

(*Curtain opens. Sarah and Granddad are playing checkers at a table. Grandma is seated in a chair, sewing.*)

SARAH, *smiling, obviously winning.* Granddad, who taught you to play checkers?

GRANDDAD. Well, I can't remember who taught me to play checkers. It was a long time ago. Why?

SARAH. I was just thinking maybe you should take a few more lessons.

GRANDDAD. Why, you young whippersnapper! What makes you think that?

SARAH. This is the fifth game we've played, Granddad, and I've won every game!

GRANDDAD. Well, that's not because I can't play checkers. It's because ... (*Tries hard to think of a reason.*) It's too dark in here. I can't see the board very well. (*Takes off glasses and looks at them.*) Yeah! And another thing, I think I need a new pair of glasses. Your grandma knows I could never play checkers in bad lighting and with old glasses!

SARAH, *sharing a grin with Grandma.* Sure, Granddad, we understand.

GRANDMA, *going to window, shivering.* It's still snowin' out there. Must be at least two feet already. (*To Sarah*) Your mom and dad are supposed to be on their way, bringing everything we need for Christmas. Hope they don't have any trouble getting here.

SARAH, *smiling.* Granddad, maybe they'll bring you a new pair of glasses! (*Granddad, peers over glasses; frowns at her.*) Grandma, I've got a question. Was Jesus really born on December 25ᵗʰ?

GRANDMA. Maybe not, but it's as good a day as any to celebrate his birth. No one really knows the exact day.

SARAH. Why didn't they write it down in the family Bible, like you do?

GRANDMA, *laughing.* Well—(*phone rings, interrupting Grandma.*)

GRANDDAD. Whew! Saved by the bell!

GRANDMA, *answering phone.* Hello? *Hello!* I can barely hear you. (*Listens for a few seconds.*) Oh, my! What? Yes, it's getting bad here too! (*Listens again.*) Sarah's fine, don't you worry about her. She'll be right here with us when you get here. Be careful. Bye. (*Turns to Sarah.*) Your mom and dad are stuck in Charleston. The roads are bad, so they're getting a room there for the night. They're not sure when they'll get here.

GRANDDAD. That's too bad. Looks like we may have Christmas a little late this year.

SARAH. Oh, well, that's all right. Jesus could have been born on December 26ᵗʰ—or the 27ᵗʰ, or even the 28ᵗʰ. Right, Grandad?

GRANDDAD. I guess that's right.

SARAH, *looking out window.* We may not have Christmas, but we do have one thing.

GRANDMA. What's that, honey?

SARAH. *Snow!* Do you know where my sled is?

GRANDMA. I think it's in the barn. We'll find it tomorrow. I might even go sledding with you!

SARAH. Okay! How about you, Granddad? You want to go, too?

GRANDDAD. Might just do that. 'Course, you'll probably have to pull the sled back up the hill for me. You know I can't see very well with my old glasses. (*Peers over glasses at Sarah.*)

SARAH, *shaking head.* Granddad, you're a sight. (*Sits up suddenly.*) I thought I heard a noise outside.

GRANDMA. It's probably just the wind. (*Goes to window.*) Surely there wouldn't be anyone traveling on a night like this.

(*Curtain closes.*)

SCENE 2

(*Passengers follow bus driver up aisle and stand in front of curtain facing audience.*)

BUS DRIVER, *at end of line, turning to face passengers.* Folks, I'm real sorry about the bus breakin' down, especially in this snowstorm, and this being Christmas Eve. I know you're all anxious to get home. I'm gonna walk into town to try to get some help.

HARRIET. What's wrong with the bus?

BUS DRIVER. I don't know. It just stopped.

LYDIA, *interrupting.* I know what's wrong with it. We probably lost something when we slid around that last curve.

MAVIS. *Lost* something? How could we *lose* something?

LYDIA. Listen here! Sometimes the brakes just fly off when you go too fast.

MAVIS. And just where, pray tell, did you learn that pearl of wisdom?

LYDIA, *slowly and proudly.* I watch the Speed Channel. Annabelle says she watches the Speed Channel too.

AMELIA. Speaking of Annabelle, where is she? (*All look around.*) Oh, there she is. (*Sees Annabelle coming up the aisle.*) Where have you been, Annabelle?

ANNABELLE. What's going on? I was sleeping. Maudine, you were supposed to wake me up when we stopped.

MAUDINE. Richard, you were supposed to wake Annabelle up when we stopped. Really, dear, you're going to have to be more responsible. I can't do everything for you!

RICHARD. Yes, dear. Sorry, Annabelle.

ANNABELLE. That's all right, Richard, but what are we doing out here anyway, making a snowman?

AUNT VERA. Harriet, you know I just love the pastor. He preaches a lot of good sermons about sin—seems he's against it—and he cooks up a real good batch of ramps, but I'm just wonderin' about him right now. Don't you think it's a weird time to be out here makin' a snowman?

HARRIET. No, Aunt Vera, we're not making a snowman. The bus broke down, and we're trying to decide what to do.

AUNT VERA. View? Yeah, Yeah, I guess it would be a nice view, 'cept I can't see much for the snow!

PASTOR. Don't you worry, Aunt Vera. And the rest of you, don't worry. I'm sure we will find out what's wrong and be on our way soon.

MAUDINE. Oh, bus driver! There's no need to go for help. My Richard is quite mec ... mech ... mech-a-nik-ally inclined. Richard, do your duty. Go and repair the bus.

RICHARD, *throwing hands in air in protest.* Maudine, I can't fix the bus. I've never repaired anything in my life!

MAUDINE. Now, dear, of course you have. Just last week you fixed the toaster, and it works like new. (*Purses lips, slightly perturbed.*) Remember, dear?

RICHARD. I just plugged it in!

MAUDINE. Well, go to the bus and plug something in!

AMELIA. John said he'd be glad to take a look at it if you want him to. Didn't you, John?

JOHN. Uh-huh.

BUS DRIVER, *eagerly.* All right, John. Are you a mechanic?

JOHN. Huh-uh.

HARRIET. It's getting awfully cold out here.

MAVIS. Yeah, what are we supposed to do until you get back with help?

LYDIA. We're all gonna freeze and never be heard of again!

ANNABELLE. I think I'll go back on the bus and take a nap.

BUS DRIVER. Now, folks, listen up. There's a real nice family lives close by—Mr. and Mrs. Miller. When we first broke down, I went to their house to use the phone, but it's not workin' now. But they said all of you could stay with them for as long as you need to. So go on over there and get warm. I'll be back as soon as I can. (*Goes out as he came in.*)

(*Everyone starts toward the cottage.*)

PASTOR, *turning to face people.* We'll be all right. We must have faith. God said he'd never leave us or forsake us, that he'd be with us all the way. (*His tone becomes lighthearted.*) God goes on bus trips, too, you know.

LYDIA, *irritated.* Next time, he can have my seat.

(*Curtain opens. Grandad, Grandma and Sarah seated as before curtain closed.*)

PASTOR, *knocks on door; greets Granddad as he opens door.* Hello, Mr. Miller. I'm Pastor Smith. Our bus driver said he talked to you about—

GRANDDAD. Yes, yes! Come in. Come in out of the cold. Warm yourselves by the fire. We've got a pot of coffee fixin'. Just make yourselves at home. This is my wife, and this is Sarah, our granddaughter.

PASTOR. We're pleased to meet you all. This is John.

GRANDDAD. Hello, John. You doin' okay?

JOHN. Uh-huh.

PASTOR. This is Amelia, Lydia, Mavis, Annabelle, Richard, and Maudine.

(*They all greet the Millers warmly.*)

MAUDINE. Hello, Sarah. How are you?

SARAH. I'm fine, thank you. I love your hat!

MAUDINE. Thank you, dear. I do get a lot of comments on my sense of fashion.

LYDIA. Yeah! That's why she wears the same dress every Christmas.

MAUDINE. Never mind her. I'll let you wear my hat sometime if you want to, Sarah.

PASTOR. And this is Aunt Vera and Harriet.

AUNT VERA. Glad to meet you. This is the first time I've ever stayed at a Holiday Inn. It's nice. Real homey.

SARAH. Holiday Inn? Grandma, this is not Holiday—

GRANDMA, *putting her hand over Sarah's mouth.* Sarah, let's go see if the coffee's ready. These folks are cold.

SARAH. But, Grandma, this is not—

GRANDMA. Come on, Sarah. (*Takes her by the hand and exits.*)

PASTOR. We really appreciate your kind hospitality.

GRANDDAD. We're glad to help anyway we can. But I have to ask, what are you folks doin' way out here on a bus on Christmas Eve?

RICHARD. We've been to Ogelby Park to see the lights and decorations—

AMELIA. And do some shopping. Right, John?

JOHN. Uh-huh.

HARRIET. And we would have been home by now if our bus hadn't broken down.

LYDIA. You mean if we hadn't "lost something."

MAVIS. Will you please be quiet about losin' something. Maybe next time we'll *lose* you!

GRANDMA, *entering with Sarah, carrying coffee and cups.* Here we are. Maybe some coffee will warm you up and help you to relax.

ANNABELLE. Good! Maybe it'll keep me awake.

AMELIA. Well, I don't think I'm gonna be able to relax. We're gonna miss Christmas. John and I always have big plans for Christmas. We even got new outdoor decorations this year, didn't we, John?

JOHN. Uh-huh.

MAUDINE. Oh, I am so glad to hear that, dear. (*To Richard.*) Now, Richard, you don't have to worry. (*To Amelia.*) Richard said to me just the other day that he wondered when you and John were going to get some new outdoor decorations. I told him that one day it would happen.

RICHARD, *aghast, protesting.* No, I didn't—

MAUDINE, *interrupting.* Richard, please be a dear and get me a cup of coffee.

RICHARD. *Sarcastically sweet.* Of course, sweetheart.

HARRIET, *going to window.* I believe it's quit snowing. Now, if the driver can get the bus fixed soon, we can be on our way. (*To Grandma.*) We're sorry to be such a bother.

AUNT VERA. Yes, honey, who is your father? I might know him.

GRANDMA. Well, uh, my father?

HARRIET. Aunt Vera, we weren't talking about her father. I said, "Sorry to be such a bother."

AUNT VERA. Oh, honey, you're no bother.

GRANDMA. As a matter of fact, it's nice to have company on Christmas Eve. Sarah's mom and dad were on their way here with Christmas and all the trimmings, but they're stuck in Charleston.

SARAH. We're waiting 'til they come to cut a tree and decorate it. They have all the presents too. But as Granddad says, "Take life as it comes, and don't get your knickers in a twist."

(*Embarrassed, Granddad and Grandma clear their throats loudly.*)

PASTOR. *Smiling.* That sounds like good advice.

MAVIS. I'd like to know whose bright idea it was in the first place to go on a bus trip this close to Christmas.

(*All heads turn toward Pastor.*)

PASTOR. I just thought it would be fun to see the lights. I hadn't planned on the bus breaking down or the bad weather.

AUNT VERA. That's right, Pastor. Bein' together—that's what Christmas is all about. I really enjoyed the Christmas program at church Friday night. My cute little preacher friend was there, you know. He comes every year.

MAUDINE. Oh, I just thought of something. I won't get to try out my new recipe for peanut butter-pinto bean casserole at the church bazaar.

RICHARD. Like the pastor says, "No matter how bad things look, there's always something to be thankful for."

ANNABELLE, *waking slightly.* Where are we?

LYDIA. Go back to sleep, Annabelle. We'll have Maudine wake you when it's time to go.

ANNABELLE. Yeah! I've heard that before.

MAVIS. We would have been home on time if Maudine hadn't had to shop in every store in the mall.

MAUDINE. I was looking for a doll for our granddaughter, Millicent. Not just any doll, either. There's a special one she just *has* to have. She can be quite demanding at times. I don't know *who* she gets that from. Anyway, *Lydia* was the one who insisted we look at the lights one more time.

LYDIA. We had time for *that.* (*Looks directly at Amelia.*) What we didn't have time for was spending three hours in the restaurant, *Amelia*!

PASTOR. Lydia's right, Amelia. We ate lunch and then got back on the bus to go, and you were in the restaurant another hour. What were you doing?

AMELIA. Well, it wasn't my fault that my cousin Louise was eating there, too. I think it's been a couple of days since we last talked, and we had a lot to catch up on. I couldn't just *not* talk to her, could I, John?

JOHN, *emphatically.* Huh-uh.

SARAH, *going to John.* Would you like a cookie, John?

JOHN, *taking cookie.* Uh-huh.

SARAH. Would you like a cup of coffee?

JOHN. Huh-uh.

SARAH, *turning to Amelia.* Does he say anything else?

AMELIA. Huh-uh.

(Sarah turns to walk away and shrugs her shoulders.)

GRANDMA, *bringing Bible to Granddad.* Henry, don't you think this would be a good time to read the Christmas story?

GRANDDAD. Yes, Mama, I sure do. *(Takes the Bible.)*

SARAH. Every Christmas Eve Granddad reads the story of baby Jesus.

GRANDDAD. Before I read, I just want to say that I know you are all disappointed that you're not with your families this evening, but we feel blessed that the Lord sent you here to be with us.

SARAH. Granddad, may I give them something?

GRANDDAD. You sure can.

SARAH, *giving everyone a Christmas card.* Here. I made these, and I hope they make you feel better.

(Everyone reads cards and is visibly moved with appreciation.)

PASTOR. Thank you very much, Sarah. That's very sweet of you.

SARAH. You're welcome. *(Turns to John.)* How about you? Do you feel better?

JOHN. Uh-huh.

(*Sarah smiles and sits down to listen to Granddad read.*)

GRANDDAD. "And it came to pass, in those days ..."

(*Curtain closes.*)

Scene 3

Nativity

(*Curtain opens with Joseph, Mary, and baby Jesus on center stage. Narrator reads all scripture from offstage.*)

NARRATOR, *reading Luke 2:1–7.* And it came to pass in those days, that there went out a decree from Caesar Augustus, that all the world should be taxed. (And this taxing was first made when Cyrenius was governor of Syria.) And all went to be taxed, every one into his own city. And Joseph also went up from Galilee, out of the city of Nazareth, into Judaea, unto the city of David, which is called Bethlehem; (because he was of the house and lineage of David:) To be taxed with Mary his espoused wife, being great with child. And so it was, that, while they were there, the days were accomplished that she should be delivered. And she brought forth her firstborn son, and wrapped him in swaddling clothes, and laid him in a manger; because there was no room for them in the inn.

(*"What Child Is This?" is played or sung.*)

NARRATOR, *reading Luke 2:8.* And there were in the same country shepherds abiding in the field, keeping watch over their flock by night.

(*Shepherds walk up aisle toward stage; they huddle at front, just off stage right.*)

NARRATOR, *reading Luke 2:9–12.* And, lo, the angel of the Lord came upon them, and the glory of the Lord shone round about them: and they were sore afraid. And the angel said unto them, Fear not: for, behold, I bring you good tidings of great joy, which shall be to all people. For unto you is born this day in the city of David a Saviour, which is Christ the Lord. And this shall be a sign unto you; Ye shall find the babe wrapped in swaddling clothes, lying in a manger.

(*An angel appears to the shepherds, who are frightened.*)

NARRATOR, *reading Luke 2:13–14.* And suddenly there was with the angel a multitude of the heavenly host praising God, and saying, Glory to God in the highest, and on earth peace, good will toward men.

(*A multitude of angels join first angel.*)

NARRATOR, *reading Luke 2:15.* And it came to pass, as the angels were gone away from them into heaven, the shepherds said one to another, Let us now go even unto Bethlehem, and see this thing which is come to pass, which the Lord hath made known unto us.

(*Angels stand behind Mary, Joseph, and Jesus at back center stage.*)

NARRATOR, *reading Luke 2:16.* And they came with haste, and found Mary, and Joseph, and the babe lying in a manger.

(*Shepherds quickly enter stage right, beside the manger.*)

NARRATOR, *reading Matthew 2:1–2.* Now when Jesus was born in Bethlehem of Judaea in the days of Herod the king, behold, there came wise men from the east to Jerusalem, Saying, Where is he that is born King of the Jews? for we have seen his star in the east, and are come to worship him.

(*As song "We Three Kings" is played, the wise men come slowly up aisle toward stage, stopping at stage left, beside the manger. Each carries a gift.*)

NARRATOR, *reading Matthew 2:11.* And when they were come into the house, they saw the young child with Mary his mother, and fell down, and worshipped him: and when they had opened their treasures, they presented unto him gifts; gold, and frankincense, and myrrh.

(*Wise men kneel one at a time, present gifts to Jesus, and then stand.*)

NARRATOR, *reading John 3:16–17.* For God so loved the world, that he gave his only begotten Son, that whosoever believeth on him should not perish, but have everlasting life. For God sent not his Son into the world to condemn the world; but that the world through him might be saved.

(*"O Holy Night" is sung as solo. Curtain closes.*)

Scene 4

(*Curtain opens on Miller living room; characters in same position as when Granddad began reading.*)

RICHARD. Mr. Miller, I have never heard the Christmas story read any better. It brought tears to my eyes.

MAUDINE. Mine, too. (*Sniffs and looks for tissue in purse*)

LYDIA. I know what you mean, Richard. I felt I was right there in the stable with Mary and Joseph and the baby.

AMELIA. And I could almost hear the angels singing.

HARRIET. It was wonderful! (*Looks at Annabelle.*) Annabelle would have enjoyed it too, if she had been awake.

AUNT VERA. Cake? You mean they serve cake this late here at Holiday Inn? Thank you all the same, but I don't think I want any cake.

HARRIET. Not cake, Aunt Vera. She said "awake." Oh, never mind.

MAVIS. You know, just as things haven't gone the way we planned on this trip, things probably didn't go the way Mary and Joseph planned either. I'm sure they didn't plan on having the baby Jesus in a stable and laying Him in a manger.

PASTOR. But that's how it worked out because God has his own plans. If our bus hadn't broken down, we might never have met Mr. and Mrs. Miller and Sarah. We're all very grateful to you. God bless you.

GRANDMA. Sarah, bedtime, dear. Tell everyone good night.

SARAH, *getting up.* Good night, everybody.

GRANDMA. If you ladies will come with us, we'll show you where you can sleep.

(*Women get up; follow Grandma.*)

MAUDINE, *passing Annabelle.* Annabelle, Annabelle, it's time to wake up and go to sleep.

(*Annabelle lazily follows. Grandma brings in blankets and gives them to Granddad.*)

GRANDDAD. You men will have to find you a chair or place and do the best you can. Grab a blanket, and I'll just join you. This is what I call "adventure sleepin'."

AUNT VERA, *sticking head back through door.* Good night, everybody. Sleep tight, and don't let the bedbugs bite.

(*Curtain remains open, but lights grow dim. Everyone on stage is asleep.*)

(*Sometime during night, Amelia and Maudine quietly enter and awaken John and Richard. They whisper instructions. Other women except Grandma look on from back door. John and Richard wake Pastor and whisper to him. The men put on coats and exit down aisle. Women return to back room.*)

(*Curtain closes.*)

SCENE 5

(*Curtain opens on Miller's living room. At center stage is a Christmas tree, all trimmed, with packages underneath. Men are sleeping.*)

SARAH, *entering from back; sees tree and yells loudly.* Granddad! Grandma! Come here! Wake up! Come here quick!

GRANDDAD, *seeing tree.* Well, what in the world ...

GRANDMA, *entering, followed by other women.* Where did that come from? It wasn't here last night!

SARAH. Isn't it beautiful? Look, Grandma, this has your name on it. (*Hands a present to Grandma.*) This one's for you, Granddad! And this one's for *me!*

GRANDDAD, *looking suspiciously at others.* I think there must have been some Christmas rats scurrying around last night.

RICHARD, *looking at Pastor.* I didn't hear a thing. How about you, John? You hear anything?

JOHN. Huh-uh.

(*There's a knock at the door. Maudine answers.*)

BUS DRIVER. Morning, folks. Good news! Bus is all fixed, and the roads are clear. We can get started home. By the way, I'm sorry to tell you all this, but it looks like somebody took some packages off the bus during the night—

MAUDINE, *interrupting bus driver.* Shh! Okay, folks. You heard the bus driver. Come on, let's go.

(*They grab their coats, say their goodbyes and thank-yous. As they follow the bus driver down the aisle, they look back to see Granddad, Grandma, and Sarah opening presents. Sarah holds up a doll for Grandma and Granddad to see. She holds it close and then puts on Maudine's hat. They all proceed down aisle toward door.*)

MAUDINE, *sweetly, taking Richard's arm.* Oh, Richard, did you buy *me* a Christmas present?

RICHARD. As a matter of fact, Maudine, I did.

MAUDINE. Oh, I'm gonna open it as soon as I get home! (*Rubs hands together excitedly.*)

RICHARD. I'm afraid you can't.

MAUDINE. And just why not?

RICHARD. Because I put it in there under the Millers' tree.

MAUDINE. Oh, Richard! Well, I guess that's ok. But, of course, now you'll have to buy me another one, or two, or three. (*They exit.*)

RICHARD. (*Speaks loudly from outside door.*) Yes, dear!

End

Flossie's No Bother

Characters

Aunt Vera: Elderly lady, nearly deaf
Flossie: Vera's sister
Pastor: Church pastor
Amelia: Friend of Aunt Vera
John: Amelia's husband
Maudine: Friend of Vera
Richard: Maudine's husband
Bernie: Vera's brother
Violet: Bernie's wife
Mavis: Friend of Vera
Lydia: Mavis's sister
Helen: Lydia's neighbor
Annabelle: Sleepy friend of Vera
Hank: Construction worker
Vickie: Young neighbor of Vera, age 8-12
Larry: Vickie's cousin, age 8-12
Bob: Larry's dad
Narrator
Mary
Joseph
Shepherds
Angels
Wise men

Scene 1

NARRATOR. *Speaking in front of closed curtain to audience.* Vera's sister, Flossie, has been living with their brother, Bernie, and his wife, Violet. Since Vera and Flossie haven't seen each other for a while, Bernie has decided that now, just before Christmas, would be the perfect time to bring Flossie to Vera's for a nice, long visit. Is Bernie being a thoughtful brother—or does he have an ulterior motive? *Exits as curtain opens.*

(*Aunt Vera sits in her rocker. Her glasses are on a chain around her neck. Doorbell rings. Aunt Vera goes to door. There stand Bernie, Violet, and Flossie, with luggage.*)

AUNT VERA. Well, land sakes! Look who's here! It's brother Bernie and Violet. Well, it can't be—it's my own sister, Flossie! Come in! Come in! (*She hugs them all.*) Sit down. What brings you all to this neck of the woods? (*Notices luggage*) Are you taking a trip?

BERNIE. No, Vera, we came to see you.

AUNT VERA. Oh, you've been to the zoo! That's nice. I've always liked going to the zoo. (*She speaks* dreamily.) I especially like the cute little monkeys.

VIOLET. No, Vera, not the zoo, dear. He said we've come to see *you.* Don't you remember? We called and told you we were bringing Flossie to stay with you for a while. Don't you remember?

AUNT VERA. Why, sure, I remember. I wouldn't forget a thing like that. By the way, does anyone see my glasses? I forgot what I did with my glasses.

BERNIE. Here they are, Vera. (*Removes the glasses from around Vera's neck and reaches them to her. She puts them on.*) We thought we would spend the night with you and head home in the morning. We've made some plans of our own, but Flossie will be staying with you a little longer.

FLOSSIE, *whining.* If it's no bother. I don't ever want to be a bother.

AUNT VERA. Land sakes! Of course it's no bother. Bernie, put her things in the green room, and you and Violet can have the blue one. Girls, grab you a chair and sit a spell.

VIOLET. You two visit while I help Bernie put the things away. (*Exits with Bernie.*)

FLOSSIE. I just brought a few clothes, Vera. I hope it won't take up too much room in your closet. I wouldn't want to take up too much room in your closet.

AUNT VERA. Don't you fret about that, dear. I'm just so glad you decided to come visit.

FLOSSIE. It's always good to see you, Vera. But I have to be honest—you know Papa always told us to be honest—it really wasn't my idea to come visit.

AUNT VERA. What do you mean?

FLOSSIE. Oh, not that I didn't want to come visit, but I think Bernie and Violet are getting tired of me being underfoot all the time. I'm getting to be a bother, especially at Christmas. They have a lot to do and places to go.

AUNT VERA. Places with snow? You mean they're going someplace where there's snow? There's enough snow around here for me. But that's fine. We'll just enjoy each other's company.

FLOSSIE. Just so I'm not a bother. I don't ever want to be a bother.

(Bernie and Violet reenter the room.)

AUNT VERA. Make yourselves at home. How about something to drink? I've got some hot chocolate already made.

BERNIE. Hot chocolate sounds yummy.

AUNT VERA. Tummy? Oh! I'm sorry, dear. What's wrong with your tummy?

VIOLET. No, Vera. There's nothing wrong with his tummy. He said, "Yummy!"

AUNT VERA. If his tummy's not feeling well, this hot chocolate will be good for it. Flossie, would you like to help me in the kitchen? *(They exit.)*

(Bernie and Violet walk to front center stage.)

BERNIE. Now remember, Vi, you can't say a word to anyone about what's *really* going on. Mum's the word. *(Both put fingers to lips.)*

(Curtain closes.)

Scene 2

(Maudine enters, walks up the aisle, and stops in front of closed curtain.)

MAUDINE. *Looking back toward the door.* Richard, do hurry, dear. I will not have you make us late for a social function. People don't expect me to be late for a social function. I know they're anxious to see my new dress and matching hat. *(Richard enters from back door and walks up aisle.)* Richard, where have you been?

RICHARD. I was helping that poor man pick up his packages. Someone *(looks sternly at Maudine)* blew the horn and nearly scared the life out of him. His packages went everywhere.

MAUDINE. I merely wanted him to know we were there, Richard. I probably saved his life. Next time he won't walk so close to traffic.

RICHARD. Maudine, he was on the sidewalk.

MAUDINE. Never mind, Richard. Come on, we're gonna be late.

RICHARD, *hesitating.* Wait, Maudine. I've been thinking. If Flossie's sick, she may not want company.

MAUDINE. She's not sick, dear. Vera just wanted to have a little party to cheer her up. It seems Bernie doesn't want Flossie living with them anymore. He's throwing her out, and right at Christmas!

RICHARD. Aw, I'm sure that's not the case.

MAUDINE. Yes, that *is* the case, but of course you would take up for him. After all, he is one of your kind. I heard he wouldn't even let her take her clothes with her.

RICHARD. Maybe you could give her some of your fashionable ensembles.

MAUDINE. I would, Richard. You know I'm noted for my generous donations to worthy causes. But it wouldn't work. She wouldn't have the matching accessories.

RICHARD. Well, maybe you could give her some of your matching—

MAUDINE, *looking at watch and interrupting.* Oh, my goodness, look at the time! Come along, Richard. We're late.

RICHARD. Coming along, dear. (*Both go behind closed curtain at stage left.*)

(*John and Amelia enter and start up the aisle toward closed curtain.*)

AMELIA, I brought this chicken casserole. It's always been one of Flossie's favorites. Do you think this will be enough, John?

JOHN. Uh-huh.

AMELIA. I don't know. Maybe I should have brought more. Do you think I should have brought more?

JOHN. Huh-uh.

AMELIA. I feel so sorry for Flossie. Maudine told me that she's lost weight, that she's nothing but skin and bones. But it's no wonder. Maudine said that Bernie only allowed her one meal a day. And she had to use paper plates and plastic forks. That's just terrible, isn't it, John?

JOHN. Uh-huh.

AMELIA. Now, don't take that tone with me! I know you like Bernie, and he's your friend, but I can tell by the way you're talking you're taking up for him. Would you want me to fix you just one meal a day?

JOHN. *Huh-uh!*

AMELIA. Then you just watch what you're saying. (*Both go behind closed curtain at stage left.*)

(*Mavis and Annabelle, carrying cookies, enter and start up the aisle toward closed curtain.*)

ANNABELLE, Thanks for picking me up, Mavis. I was just taking a nap when you called. I already had some cookies made, so I brought some of them. Where's Lydia? Doesn't she usually come with you?

MAVIS. She's not coming. I called her, and she said she has a headache. It's strange, though. Her headaches usually happen only after I have driven her somewhere. If I didn't know better, I'd think she might not like my driving.

ANNABELLE. Vera said she was having this get-together to help make Flossie feel better. I guess she's been feeling poorly.

MAVIS. Haven't you heard? Bernie threw her out of the house. Told her she had to go live with Vera. You know, he used to spend all his time in that store. I don't know what he's up to now.

ANNABELLE. He must be up to something. Men are always up to something.

MAVIS. You know he never would take her anywhere—no concerts or any kind of trips.

ANNABELLE. Well, that's a shame. I do some of my best sleeping on trips. I slept so good on that bus trip we took last Christmas.

MAVIS. Tell you what. Next trip I go on, you and Flossie can go with me, and you can sleep all you want.

ANNABELLE. That sounds great! (*Both go behind closed curtain at stage left.*

Scene 3

(*Curtain opens. Lydia, Helen, Mavis, and Flossie are seated. Annabelle snoozes in chair. Flossie is busily knitting. Others are milling around a table of food.*)

MAVIS. I see you made it after all, Lydia. I thought you weren't coming. Is your head feeling better?

LYDIA. Much better, thank you. I got to feeling better right after you called. My neighbor, Helen, happened to be coming this way, so she brought me.

MAVIS. Glad to meet you, Helen. (*Turns to Lydia.*) I'm so glad you're feeling better. I'd hate for you to miss the party because of a headache.

HELEN, *to Lydia.* I thought you told me your sister wasn't coming to the party so you didn't have a way to come.

LYDIA. Oh, did I say that? That must have been when my head was *really* hurting.

AMELIA, *going to Flossie.* What are you making, Flossie? Can I see?

FLOSSIE. Sure. I've been working on something to keep me busy so I won't be a bother. I don't ever want to be a bother. (*Holds up a weird-looking sweater.*)

AMELIA. Well, that's real nice. Isn't that nice, John?

JOHN. Uh-huh.

FLOSSIE. I'll do most of it, and then I'll give it to Vera to finish.

AUNT VERA, *suddenly alert.* No, thank you. I don't want any spinach. Flossie, you know I never could stand spinach. (*Takes John's arm.*) But we have some good-looking cookies over here. I think they're potato and raisin cookies. (*Picks up plate and shows cookies to John.*) Would you like to have one of these?

JOHN. Huh-uh!

RICHARD. Pretty lively party, isn't it, Annabelle? (*Notices Annabelle is asleep,*) Well, maybe not.

(*Door opens. Vickie sticks her head in*)

VICKIE. Aunt Vera! (*Louder*) Aunt Vera!

AUNT VERA. Yes, child. Come in. (*Vickie and Larry enter.*) You all remember Vickie from next door. Who's this with you, honey?

VICKIE. This is my cousin, Larry. He's spending Christmas with us.

AUNT VERA. Well, hello, Cousin Harry!

LARRY, *correcting Vera.* Larry. My name's Larry, ma'am.

AUNT VERA. Oh, I'm sorry. That's a good name, Perry. (*Larry rolls eyes as Vera continues dreamily,*) Perry Como was one of my favorite singers. (*Turns to Maudine.*) You know I almost married him when I was young.

MAUDINE, *gasping.* You almost married *Perry Como? The* Perry Como? Well, what happened? Why didn't you marry him?

AUNT VERA. He never asked me.

(*Maudine rolls eyes.*)

VICKIE. Aunt Vera, could we borrow some sugar? Mom's making cookies and ran out.

AUNT VERA. Yes, indeed. I'll go get some for you. (*Aunt Vera exits.*)

VICKIE, *walking toward the Christmas tree, turning to Flossie.* Your tree is beautiful! But I think there's something missing. (*Looks at Larry.*) Right?

LARRY. Right!

AUNT VERA, *returning with sugar.* Here you go. If you need any more, just come back.

VICKIE. Thanks, Aunt Vera. (*Starts to leave.*)

LARRY, *coaxing Vickie to center stage.* I still don't believe what you told me.

VICKIE. It's true. I wouldn't make it up. You'll find out. Come on. I'll show you. (*They stand in front of John.*) Excuse me, sir. Is your name John?

JOHN. Uh-huh.

VICKIE, *nudging Larry.* Now it's your turn.

LARRY, *looking from Vickie back to John.* Sir, are you a hundred years old?

JOHN. Huh-uh.

VICKIE. See? I told you. That's all he ever says. (*To Aunt Vera.*) Thanks for the sugar. We'll be right back with a special surprise. (*Children exit; everyone looks questioningly at each other.*)

LYDIA. Maudine, I love your new dress.

MAUDINE. Why, thank you, Lydia. Nice of you to notice.

LYDIA, *to Mavis.* I bought me some bedroom curtains just like that last week.

MAUDINE. (*Overhears and is appalled.*) Well!

RICHARD. Oh, by the way, Vera, I saw Bernie the other day. He has put on some weight and is really looking good! (*All the women except*

Aunt Vera and Flossie give Richard a dirty look. Flossie dabs at her eyes.)

AUNT VERA. There, there, dear. It'll be all right. Richard didn't mean to upset you. (*Goes to Richard and smacks his hand.*) Did you, Richard?

RICHARD. What did I say? What did I say?

(*Knock is heard at door.*)

AMELIA. Vera, dear. Someone's at the door.

AUNT VERA. More! You want more? Oh, honey, get all you want. There's all kinds of food over there.

AMELIA. No, Aunt Vera, door, someone's at the … never mind, dear. I'll get it. (*Answers door.*) It's the pastor.

AUNT VERA. Come on in, Pastor. Get you something to eat. Look, Flossie, it's the pastor. You remember him, don't you?

FLOSSIE. Yes, I think so. How are you, Pastor?

PASTOR. Fine, thank you. It's good to see you again, Flossie. I hear you're gonna be with us for Christmas.

FLOSSIE. Yes, but don't let me get in the way. I never want to be a bother.

PASTOR. Oh, you couldn't be a bother. Look, I can't stay. I was working on the stage at church, and I need some help. Richard, can you help me?

RICHARD, *jumping up quickly.* I would love to! How about you, John? Do you need to help too?

JOHN. *Uh-huh!*

(*John and Richard exit.*)

MAUDINE. Oh, Pastor, before you go, could we see you just a minute?

PASTOR. Sure, what is it? (*Goes to women who are in a huddle, except for Flossie and Vera.*)

MAVIS. We think there's something you should know.

PASTOR. Oh! Is something wrong?

LYDIA. Bernie threw Flossie out of his house.

AMELIA. And he's not been feeding her very well.

MAUDINE. And she doesn't have anything to wear! He got rid of all her clothes!

ANNABELLE. We heard he wouldn't even let her take naps.

PASTOR. That's all very hard to believe. But I'll talk to Bernie and see what I can find out.

MAUDINE. Thank you, Pastor. Even though you're one of "them," we feel we can count on you.

PASTOR. Thank you, I think. I'll get back to you. (*Exits.*)

(*As Pastor is leaving, Vickie sticks her head in.*)

VICKIE, *yelling.* Aunt Vera! (*Louder.*) Aunt Vera!

AUNT VERA. Yes, child. Come in.

VICKIE. We brought you a star.

AUNT VERA. Hey, everybody, Vickie bought me a car!

VICKIE. No! We brought you a star for your tree. That's what was missing. Remember?

LARRY. And we brought some presents for you and Aunt Flossie. We'll put 'em over here.

AUNT VERA. Oh, my goodness! How precious! Thank you so much.

VICKIE. We have to get back home. Merry Christmas, everybody! (*Grabs a cookie on the way out.*)

LARRY. Yeah, Merry Christmas. (*Grabs a cookie on the way out.*)

(*Knock is heard at the door as children start toward it.*)

VICKIE. I'll get it!

BOB, *Surprised to see the children.* So here you are! We wondered where you two had gone. (*Looks to Aunt Vera.*) Hello, I'm Bob, Larry's dad. I hope they haven't been any trouble. We thought they got lost.

AUNT VERA. Glad to meet you, Rob. No, there's no cost. The cookies are free. Here, have one.

BOB, *looking confused.* Uh … thank you. (*Speaks to children.*) We'd better go. Everybody's ready to go caroling. (*Shakes Vera's hand.*) Have a very Merry Christmas. (*Shakes Flossie's hand.*) Merry Christmas to you. (*Looks to other women.*) Merry Christmas, ladies. (*Bob exits with children.*)

HELEN. Wasn't that a nice young man?

MAUDINE. Yes, it's quite refreshing to see one of them turn out like that.

AUNT VERA. Girls, is everything ready at the church for the program Sunday?

AMELIA. I think so, Aunt Vera. The men are there now, painting the stage.

AUNT VERA. Old age! Oh, honey, I know all about old age! But you can't let old age stop you. You just have to think young. Hmm, speaking of young, I do hope my little preacher friend is there this year. (*She sits down.*) He's just the sweetest man.

MAVIS. Too bad they're not all sweet.

MAUDINE. Men! They do stick up for each other, don't they?

AMELIA. Annabelle, why didn't you ever get married?

ANNABELLE. I never found the right man.

LYDIA. I don't think anyone's ever found one of *them*.

HELEN. I found one of 'em. My Stanley is a good man, always helpful and polite. (*Women all look at each other, unbelieving.*)

MAVIS. That's good, but I'll bet he didn't come that way.

MAUDINE. No, they don't come that way. You have to work on them a long time to make them turn out right. I try to steer Richard in the right direction. But so many times he forgets to ask me what he should think. Amelia, is John like that?

AMELIA. Uh-huh!

MAVIS, *looking at Flossie.* Oh, look at poor Flossie. She looks so pitiful.

LYDIA. She looks like she's lost fifty pounds in the last week.

ANNABELLE. I think her hair is getting grayer too—and thinner. That's one of the signs of malnutrition, you know.

MAUDINE. She probably needs new glasses too. Her eyes must be getting worse. She didn't say a word about my new dress.

AMELIA. She always loved my chicken casserole, but she didn't eat any of it.

MAUDINE. Well, dear, it *was* a bit heavy on the garlic.

AMELIA, *indignantly.* What do you mean? I thought it was just right!

(*A knock is heard at door.*)

FLOSSIE. Vera, I think there's someone at the door.

AUNT VERA. Floor? We dropped something on the floor?

FLOSSIE. No, dear. Not floor—door. I'll see who it is. I've been sittin' here too long anyway. (*Goes to door.*) Yes?

HANK. Good evening, ma'am. My name's Hank. I'm looking for Bernie. Is he here?

FLOSSIE. No, Bernie's not here. Why are you looking for him? Is he in trouble?

HANK. No, we're doing some work for him at his house. We've run into a problem, and I need to talk to him about it.

FLOSSIE. No, I'm sorry. He's not here, and I have no idea where he is.

HANK. Well, sorry to bother you. We'll keep on looking. (*Hank exits.*)

(*Flossie closes door and sits down.*)

AUNT VERA. I couldn't find anything on the floor, Flossie.

FLOSSIE. No, dear, there's nothing on the floor. It was a young man at the door, looking for Bernie.

AUNT VERA. Oh, okay. Bernie's not here, dear.

MAUDINE. Well! Can you believe *that?*

AMELIA. What?

MAUDINE. Didn't you hear what that man, Hank, said? Bernie's redoing Flossie's room so he can rent it out!

MAVIS. Are you sure?

MAUDINE. We just heard it with our own ears!

ANNABELLE. That's terrible! I never thought Bernie would treat his own sister that way!

LYDIA. Well, after all, he is a man.

(*Door opens. Richard and John enter.*)

RICHARD, *happily.* We got the stage all ready for the program. You girls been having a good time visiting?

MAUDINE, *standing abruptly.* Richard, you men are all alike! (*Sweetly says her goodbyes to Vera and Flossie.*) Come on, we're going home! (*Pushes him toward door.*)

AMELIA, *gruffly.* John, is the car started?

JOHN. Uh-huh.

AMELIA. Now watch it! You've said enough already! Let's go. (*They say their goodbyes to Vera and Flossie. Amelia pushes John out the door.*)

(*Other women rise to leave as curtain closes.*)

Scene 4

NARRATOR. *Speaks to audience in front of closed curtain.* Everyone is again gathered at Aunt Vera's house just before the church Christmas program.

(*Curtain opens.*)

RICHARD. I hope we're not gonna be late for the program. Did the Pastor say why he wanted us all to be here, Vera?

AUNT VERA. He just said it was something important. Wonder where he is?

(*Door opens, and Pastor looks in.*)

PASTOR, *looking around.* Good, it looks like everybody's here. (*Everyone looks at each other, puzzled.*) I brought somebody with me. (*Bernie and Violet enter.*) They have something to tell you. (*Women look away, disinterested.*) Go ahead, Bernie.

BERNIE. Flossie, we wanted to do something special for you this Christmas.

VIOLET. You always help us out in so many ways. And we love you!

BERNIE. You know how you've always wanted your own place. While you've been here visiting Vera, we've added some rooms to our house. Now you have your own home in our home. Do you like that?

FLOSSIE. Oh, Bernie, I had no idea! I thought I was just such a bother.

VIOLET. We couldn't tell anyone. We wanted it to be a surprise for Christmas.

BERNIE. And another thing—next month we're taking you on a cruise while the work on the house is finished.

FLOSSIE. Oh, my goodness! A real cruise … on a real ship?

AUNT VERA. You never did take *me* on a cruise, Bernie.

BERNIE. You didn't let me finish, Vera. You're going, too.

AUNT VERA. How about that, Flossie? We're taking a boat ride. (*They dance around together.*)

FLOSSIE. Bernie, are you sure it won't be a bother. I don't ever want to be a bother.

PASTOR, *going to the other women.* How about that, ladies? Did you hear what Bernie's doing for his sisters? Sounds like he must be a pretty good brother, huh? (*Snaps his fingers.*) You know, I just got an idea for next Sunday's sermon. (*Speaks slowly and forcefully.*) "Things are not *always* what they seem." (*Women hang heads as Pastor looks at watch.*) Come on. We'd better get to the church. We have a Christmas program to put on!

AUNT VERA. You go on, Pastor. We'll meet you there.

RICHARD. Come on, everybody! Let's go to church! (*Everyone rises as curtain closes.*)

Scene 5

Nativity

(Curtain opens with Joseph, Mary, and baby Jesus on center stage. Narrator reads all scripture from offstage.)

NARRATOR, *reading Luke 2:1–7.* And it came to pass in those days, that there went out a decree from Caesar Augustus, that all the world should be taxed. (And this taxing was first made when Cyrenius was governor of Syria.) And all went to be taxed, every one into his own city. And Joseph also went up from Galilee, out of the city of Nazareth, into Judaea, unto the city of David, which is called Bethlehem; (because he was of the house and lineage of David:) To be taxed with Mary his espoused wife, being great with child. And so it was, that, while they were there, the days were accomplished that she should be delivered. And she brought forth her firstborn son, and wrapped him in swaddling clothes, and laid him in a manger; because there was no room for them in the inn.

("What Child Is This?" is played or sung.)

NARRATOR, *reading Luke 2:8.* And there were in the same country shepherds abiding in the field, keeping watch over their flock by night.

Shepherds walk up aisle toward stage; they huddle at front, just off stage right.)

NARRATOR, *reading Luke 2:9–12.* And, lo, the angel of the Lord came upon them, and the glory of the Lord shone round about them: and they were sore afraid. And the angel said unto them, Fear not: for, behold, I bring you good tidings of great joy, which shall be to all people. For unto you is born this day in the city of David a Saviour,

which is Christ the Lord. And this shall be a sign unto you; Ye shall find the babe wrapped in swaddling clothes, lying in a manger.

(*An angel appears to the shepherds, who are frightened.*)

NARRATOR, *reading Luke 2:13–14.* And suddenly there was with the angel a multitude of the heavenly host praising God, and saying, Glory to God in the highest, and on earth peace, good will toward men.

(*A multitude of angels join first angel.*)

NARRATOR, *reading Luke 2:15.* And it came to pass, as the angels were gone away from them into heaven, the shepherds said one to another, Let us now go even unto Bethlehem, and see this thing which is come to pass, which the Lord hath made known unto us.

(*Angels stand behind Mary, Joseph, and Jesus at back center stage.*)

NARRATOR, *reading Luke 2:16.* And they came with haste, and found Mary, and Joseph, and the babe lying in a manger.

(*Shepherds quickly enter stage right, beside the manger.*)

NARRATOR, *reading Matthew 2:1–2.* Matthew 2:1-2 Now when Jesus was born in Bethlehem of Judaea in the days of Herod the king, behold, there came wise men from the east to Jerusalem, Saying, Where is he that is born King of the Jews? for we have seen his star in the east, and are come to worship him.

(*As song "We Three Kings" is played, the wise men come slowly up aisle toward stage, stopping at stage left, beside the manger. Each carries a gift.*)

NARRATOR, *reading Matthew 2:11.* And when they were come into the house, they saw the young child with Mary his mother, and fell down, and worshipped him: and when they had opened their treasures, they presented unto him gifts; gold, and frankincense, and myrrh.

(Wise men kneel one at a time, present gifts to Jesus, and then stand.

NARRATOR, *reading John 3:16–17.* For God so loved the world, that he gave his only begotten Son, that whosoever believeth on him should not perish, but have everlasting life. For God sent not his Son into the world to condemn the world; but that the world through him might be saved.

("O Holy Night" is sung as solo. Curtain closes.)

Scene 6

(Amelia and John step out from behind curtain.)

AMELIA, *starting down aisle.* Oh, John, wasn't that a wonderful program? That Nativity scene was one of the best I've ever seen. You know, John, I never did believe all those things they were saying about Bernie. Did you?

JOHN. Huh-uh

AMELIA. I tried to tell them that you said Bernie was a good man, but they wouldn't listen. You know how people are.

JOHN. Uh-huh. *(They exit through door.)*

(Richard and Maudine step from behind curtain and start down aisle.)

RICHARD. Now you see, Maudine, what happens when you jump to conclusions?

MAUDINE. Yes, Richard.

RICHARD. I mean, you should always get your facts straight, and not jump to conclusions. Do you understand what I'm saying?

MAUDINE. Yes, Richard, I do. I'm not going to jump to conclusions anymore, not until I get my facts straight.

RICHARD. Good! I'm glad to hear that. (*Starts to exit down aisle.*)

MAUDINE. Oh, Richard.

RICHARD. Yes, dear, what now?

MAUDINE, *sweetly.* Richard, dear, did you hear that Bernie's going to take Flossie on a cruise?

RICHARD. Yes, I did.

MAUDINE. Isn't that nice of him?

RICHARD. Yes, very nice.

MAUDINE. I wonder why he decided to do that.

RICHARD. I guess he wanted to show Flossie that she's no bother. (*Richard again starts to exit but Maudine calls him back.*)

MAUDINE. Oh, Richard, dear, how come you never did take me on a cruise?

RICHARD. Like I said, Flossie's no bother! (*Richard walks out the door.*)

MAUDINE, *pausing to let Richard's words sink in and then following him.* Now, wait a minute! What do you mean by that? Richard, you come back here!

End

What's Missing?

Characters

Aunt Vera: Elderly lady, nearly deaf
Flossie: Vera's sister
Pastor: Church pastor
Amelia: Friend of Aunt Vera
John: Amelia's husband
Maudine: Friend of Vera
Richard: Maudine's husband
Bernie: Vera's brother
Violet: Bernie's wife
Mavis: Friend of Vera
Lydia: Mavis's sister
Charlie: Neighbor
Sue: Charlie's wife
Sally: Charlie and Sue's daughter, age8-12
Eddie: Charlie and Sue's son, age8-12
Annabelle: Sleepy friend of Vera
Officer Johnson: Policeman
Narrator
Mary
Joseph
Shepherds
Angels
Wise men

Scene 1

(*Curtain opens. Vera is sitting in living room with shawl on lap.*)

AUNT VERA. Flossie! Flossie! Come here! Quick! (*Examines shawl.*)

FLOSSIE, *entering from back*. What? What? What is it?

AUNT VERA. I've got a hole in my shawl! See! (*Pokes fist through the hole.*)

FLOSSIE. Vera, don't scare me like that! Rushin' around like that could give me a heart attack. Now, what is it?

AUNT VERA. It's my shawl. See? It's got a hole in it! My favorite one, too! I got it one year for Christmas. I've not had it that long.

FLOSSIE. When did you get it?

AUNT VERA, *thinking long and hard*. Uh, let me see … 1946. Grandma gave it to me for Christmas 1946.

FLOSSIE. Well, Vera, you know they don't make things like they used to. We'll work on it and see if we can mend it.

AUNT VERA. I'll have to fix it soon. I always wear it to the Christmas program. (*Lays the shawl aside.*) Speaking of the program, don't forget there's a meeting tomorrow at the church to discuss it. We'll have to get up early.

FLOSSIE. I love Christmas, Vera, but I wish they were more like they used to be. Remember how Papa would always read the Christmas story from the Bible that Grandpa left him?

AUNT VERA. I remember. (*Laughs.*) Remember the year he forgot to put his teeth in, and we thought he was reading the story of Moses and the Israelites? I asked him what that had to do with Christmas. (*They both laugh.*)

FLOSSIE. Oh, yes! He was not amused! By the way, whatever happened to Grandpa's Bible?

AUNT VERA. Bernie has it. He keeps it in a special box.

FLOSSIE. Oh yeah, that's right. Do you remember how people used to help each other around Christmas, Vera? It was a wonderful time of sharing and giving.

AUNT VERA. Living? Oh yes, Flossie. It's good to be living.

FLOSSIE. No, Vera. I said *giving.* I said Christmas used to be a special time for giving!

AUNT VERA. You don't have to shout! I'm not deaf! But you're right, Flossie. Papa always said, "It's better to give than to receive." This year, though, from what I've heard, seems to be a special time for taking.

FLOSSIE. What do you mean?

AUNT VERA. Didn't you hear about all the things missing from the neighborhood? (*A knock is heard at the door.*) Lots of things missing. Nobody seems to know what's going on. It's a shame, this happening here at Christmas. (*Another knock is heard.*)

FLOSSIE. Vera, didn't you hear that knock?

AUNT VERA. Of course, it's a shock. It's a shock to everybody. But things don't just disappear! (*Another knock comes at the door.*) I think there's someone at the door. (*She opens door.*) Yes, come in. Come in. It's too cold to stand outside. (*Charlie and family enter.*) Can I help you?

CHARLIE. Hello, ma'am. My name is Charlie. This is my wife, Sue, and our children, Sally and Eddie. We recently moved into the neighborhood.

AUNT VERA. I'm glad to meet you and your family, Charlie. I'm Vera, and this is my sister, Flossie.

CHARLIE, SUE, SALLY, EDDIE, *together.* Hello, Flossie.

AUNT VERA, *whispering loudly.* You'll have to speak up. Flossie doesn't hear very well.

(*Family speaks louder in unison*) Hello, Flossie.

(*Flossie rolls eyes and shakes head.*)

SUE. You're Bernie's sisters, aren't you? Charlie used to work for Bernie. He gave Charlie a job when we really needed it. Charlie has his own business now. The Lord's been good to us.

SALLY. Yeah! The Lord's been *really* good to us.

EDDIE. Shh!

SALLY. Well, he has.

EDDIE. *Whispering to Sally.* Just don't say too much. Know what I mean?

SALLY. Don't worry. I know how to keep a secret.

CHARLIE, *pushing Sally toward door.* Well, we'd better get going. Just wanted to tell you if you ever need us, we're close by.

SUE, *picking up shawl.* What a lovely shawl.

AUNT VERA. Thank you, honey. My grandmother gave that to me years ago. But look here. I'll have to mend it. It has a big hole in it.

SUE. Yes, I see that. That's a shame. (*Lays it down.*) Well, we'll see you later.

(*As Vera and Flossie follow Charlie to the door, Sue picks up shawl, hands it to Eddie, who hands it to Sally, who quickly hides it under her coat.*)

SUE, *leaving.* Bye, now. (*Charlie and his family exit.*)

AUNT VERA. Bye. You all come back.

FLOSSIE. They seem very nice. Good neighbors like that are hard to beat.

AUNT VERA. You want something to *eat*? Help yourself, dear. I think I'm going to bed. I'm plumb tuckered out. (*Notices her shawl is missing.*) Now what did I do with my shawl? I must have put it away somewhere and forgot it. I'd forget my head if it wasn't fastened on. Oh, well, I'll find it tomorrow. (*They exit the room.*)

(*Curtain closes.*)

Scene 2

(*Christmas program planning committee, Pastor, Lydia, Mavis, Annabelle, Vera, and Flossie at church awaiting arrival of others as curtain opens.*)

PASTOR. It won't be long before it's time for the Christmas program. Have you decided who's gonna do what?

LYDIA. I don't think anything's been decided yet. I thought that's what this meeting was for.

PASTOR. Well, it is. I just thought some of you might have been talking about it.

ANNABELLE. What do we need, Pastor? I'll be glad to help if I have a way to get here. I don't drive.

MAVIS. You can come with me, Annabelle. Maybe you and I can work on the scenery this year.

LYDIA. Work on the scenery? You? Did you forget you're color blind? (*Turns to Pastor.*) It *is* supposed to resemble a Nativity scene, isn't it?

PASTOR. Well, yes, that's the general idea.

LYDIA, *to Mavis.* That leaves you out!

MAVIS, *to Lydia.* What are *you* volunteering for, may I ask?

LYDIA. I thought I might be an angel this year.

MAVIS. An angel? That's a stretch! I don't think there's enough time for you to get *that* perfected.

AUNT VERA. Now, girls, be nice. (*Looks at watch.*) Where are the others? I can't be gone too long. I've got a pot of pinto beans cookin'.

FLOSSIE. Vera, I don't want to be a bother, but could we have some cornbread and onions with those beans?

AUNT VERA. Well, sure we can have some greens and some cornbread and onions too ... (*Looks at watch again.*) if the others ever get here, and we get this over with.

ANNABELLE. They may not even show up. People are afraid to leave their homes these days—so many things being taken from their houses and yards. It's terrible! And at Christmas!

(Curtain closes.)

Scene 3

(Curtain is closed through entire scene. House lights on. Bernie and Violet come up aisle and stand in front of curtains.)

VIOLET. Did you find it?

BERNIE. No, I can't find it anywhere.

VIOLET. Where did you see it last?

BERNIE. Grandpa's Bible is always on the stand in the hallway. It's coming apart, so I don't handle it much.

VIOLET. Well, I didn't lose it.

BERNIE. I didn't say you did. I just said I haven't had it out for a long time. I do remember showing it to Charlie and his family when they were here a while back. That's the last time I saw it.

VIOLET. I'm sure it will turn up ... probably where you left it.

(They go behind curtain stage left, and John and Amelia come up the aisle and stand in front of curtain.)

AMELIA, *looking at her watch.* Well, John, you know we're late.

JOHN. Uh-huh.

AMELIA. I can tell by the way you're talkin' that you're still upset, aren't you?

JOHN. Uh-huh.

AMELIA. You'll find your toolbox. You've probably just misplaced it. You know I'm always reminding you to put things back where you got 'em. Right?

JOHN. Uh-huh.

AMELIA. You were helping the new neighbors fix a door the other day. Did you leave it there?

JOHN. Huh-uh.

AMELIA. Well, don't worry about it. After all, it's old and the handle was broken. Maybe you'll get a new one for Christmas. Just don't be moping around all evening. Let's go. (*They go behind curtain stage left, Richard and Maudine come up aisle to front.*)

MAUDINE. Oh, Richard, I'm just sick!

RICHARD. Maudine, don't go on so. It's not a big deal.

MAUDINE. Not a big deal! Of course, it's a big deal! That pink flamingo has been in our front yard for over ten years! I got it for you on our thirtieth anniversary. It was slightly faded, but you loved it so. Now, it's gone!

RICHARD. *In sarcastic tone.* Yes, I hate that. That's too bad. I could almost cry.

MAUDINE. I don't know what happened to it, but if we don't find it, I'll get you another one just like it, dear.

RICHARD. *Again, sarcastically.* Oh, that would be more than I could ever hope for.

MAUDINE. Our new neighbors were admiring it the other day. I think they were impressed with my knowledge of yard decor.

RICHARD. *Again, in sarcastic tone.* I'm sure they were, dear. Most people are usually quite impressed with your knowledge.

MAUDINE. What a sweet thing for you to say, Richard. (*Looks at watch.*) Oh, goodness, we're late. Come along.

RICHARD. Coming along, dear. (*They go behind curtain at stage left.*)

Scene 4

(*Curtain opens on meeting at church with everyone present.*)

PASTOR. While we were waiting for everyone to get here, we went ahead and made some decisions for the program. I hope that's all right with everyone.

AUNT VERA. Yeah, I've gotta get home soon and see about my beans. I hope they haven't burned.

MAVIS. I'm going to have to go, too. Where have you all been? This meeting was supposed to have started an hour ago.

ANNABELLE, *yawning.* It's way past my nap time.

VIOLET. We were late because Bernie has mislaid his grandfather's Bible.

BERNIE. I didn't mislay it.

FLOSSIE. Oh, Bernie, you lost Grandfather's Bible? Where did you lose it?

BERNIE. Well, if I knew that, it wouldn't be lost, would it?

AUNT VERA, *softly.* Now, Bernie, don't yell at your sister. It's not her fault you lost Grandfather's Bible.

(Bernie rolls his eyes and shakes his head.)

AMELIA. John made us late.

RICHARD. How's that, John? How's that your fault?

(John opens mouth to speak, but Amelia speaks before John can.)

AMELIA. He lost his toolbox.

PASTOR, *to John.* Where'd you have it last?

(John opens mouth to speak, but Amelia cuts him off.)

AMELIA. He thinks he may have left it at the neighbor's house. He was helping them fix a door. Anyway, he's not going to mope about it this evening, are you, John?

JOHN. Huh-uh.

MAUDINE. We were late because Richard lost his pink flamingo.

(Everyone looks at each other, puzzled.)

MAVIS. Your pink flamingo?

RICHARD. Actually, I didn't lose it. It just mysteriously disappeared from our front yard.

ANNABELLE. Does it nest there?

MAUDINE. Oh, Annabelle, it's not a real flamingo. It's a plastic one I got for Richard for our anniversary. It's upset him so that it's missing. He's been acting really quite strangely.

PASTOR. In what way?

MAUDINE. He just stares out the front window and smiles all the time. I'm getting worried about him.

FLOSSIE. I've heard about cases like that.

AUNT VERA, *cupping her ear.* Places like what?

FLOSSIE. Not places. Cases. I think Richard has separation anxiety. It happens mostly with men. They get emotionally attached to something, and when it's gone, they just stare and smile.

AUNT VERA. Flossie, you've been watching too much Dr. Phil. Come on, let's go see about those beans.

FLOSSIE. Okay. (*They leave. Everyone else gets up to leave, but continues talking.*)

BERNIE. It seems like everyone in the neighborhood is missing something.

LYDIA. Everybody but me, I guess. I haven't noticed anything missing.

(*Everyone stops abruptly and looks at each other.*)

MAUDINE. Oh really, Lydia? You're the only one not missing anything? Some of us might find that rather interesting. Don't you find that interesting, Richard?

RICHARD, *holding up hands.* Now, leave me out of this.

LYDIA. Maudine, are you accusing me of something?

(*Maudine shrugs shoulders, but says nothing.*)

RICHARD. There you go again, Maudine, jumping to conclusions.

PASTOR. Yes, let's be careful what we say. I just hope and pray this will all be cleared up soon. Good night, everybody. (*They all leave.*)

(*Curtain closes.*)

Scene 5

(*Curtain opens at Aunt Vera's house before the program. Cookies and hot chocolate are on table. Everyone is present.*)

AUNT VERA. I'm glad all of you could come this evening. And all these goodies you brought look so yummy. Help yourselves, everybody.

VIOLET. I'm looking forward to the program. It gets better every year.

AMELIA. I think so too, but after all, the Christmas story never gets old, just more precious every year.

RICHARD. I think Mavis and Annabelle did a great job on the scenery. Don't you, John?

JOHN. Uh- huh.

MAVIS. Thank you, Richard.

BERNIE. I can't say I've ever seen those colors in the Nativity scene before ... but I like it!

(*Mavis and Annabelle give thumbs-up to each other.*)

ANNABELLE. I've got an idea. Why don't we all go caroling one night?

PASTOR. That sounds great! We all like to sing.

AUNT VERA. You heard the phone ring? Get it, will you, Flossie?

FLOSSIE. No, Vera, the phone didn't ring. The pastor said, "Sing."

AUNT VERA. Okay! (*Starts singing "Joy to the World" until she notices everyone staring. She gradually stops as she notices nobody else is singing.*)

MAUDINE. Richard and I can't go caroling. We can't be gone from the house too long. Something else might come up missing. We still haven't found Richard's pink flamingo.

RICHARD. No, and I really, *really* hate that.

AMELIA. I know what you mean, Maudine. I'm hoping the program doesn't last too long tonight. We just feel safer at home, don't we, John?

JOHN. Uh-huh.

MAVIS. Have any of the missing items turned up?

EVERYONE. No!

LYDIA. Wait a minute. My rocking chair turned up!

(*Everyone stares at her.*)

MAUDINE. What do you mean, your rocking chair turned up? I thought you didn't have anything missing.

LYDIA. I didn't until last Tuesday. I noticed my old rocking chair with the broken rocker was gone from the front porch. Then, on Saturday, it was back—as good as new!

VIOLET. Now that is *really* a mystery.

MAUDINE, *looking doubtful.* Yes, isn't it?

(*Knock sounds on door. Everyone silent on stage. Vera, oblivious to the knock, adjusts her clothes as another knock is heard.*)

BERNIE. Vera, there's someone at the door. Never mind. I'll get it. (*Opens door.*) Yes, Officer, can we help you?

OFFICER. (*Stepping inside.*) I'm looking for Pastor Smith. Is he here?

PASTOR. Here I am. What's going on?

OFFICER. I was driving past the church tonight, and I saw someone taking the baby Jesus from the outdoor manger scene. As I was taking him to jail, he told me a story I think you should hear. (*Looks around.*) Maybe *all* of you will want to hear.

PASTOR. Bernie, bring him in. Let's see what's this all about.

OFFICER, *motions to Charlie and family, who are standing behind him.* Come in, all of you. Go ahead. Tell 'em what you told me.

AUNT VERA. Why, it's Charlie and his family, my new neighbors.

AMELIA. Yes, John helped him fix his door. Didn't you, John?

JOHN. Uh-huh.

BERNIE. I showed Grandpa's Bible to him.

MAUDINE. They were admiring Richard's pink flamingo just before it went missing.

RICHARD. Charlie, do you know anything about these missing items?

OFFICER. Now, wait a minute! I told you he has something to tell you.

PASTOR. Yes, let's listen to Charlie.

CHARLIE. I wasn't *taking* the baby Jesus.

EDDIE. No, he was putting it back.

FLOSSIE. What do you mean, putting it back? Where was it?

SALLY. We took it to fix the broken arm. We were putting it back when the officer came by.

PASTOR. Oh, I see!

AMELIA. What about John's toolbox? Have you seen it?

SUE. Charlie noticed the handle was broken, so he took it to repair it. It's outside in the car. We were bringing it back, too.

SALLY, *walks over to Bernie.* We took your Bible and got it all put together like new. It was really falling apart. I'll bring it in to you. (*She exits.*)

LYDIA. Were you the one who fixed my rocking chair?

CHARLIE. Yes, Eddie and I did that together.

(*Sally brings in the Bible and gives it to Bernie and gives Vera's shawl to Sue.*)

AUNT VERA. That's my shawl. I've been looking all over for it, haven't I, Flossie? Tell 'em. I've been looking all over for it.

FLOSSIE. Yes, she's been looking all over for it.

SUE, *putting shawl around Aunt Vera's shoulders.* I noticed a hole in it when we were here, so I mended it for you.

EDDIE. Mom is real good at mending things.

AUNT VERA, *admiring shawl.* Land sakes! It's just like new! Look, Flossie, it's just like new!

MAUDINE. I'd like to know what you've done with Richard's pink flamingo.

CHARLIE. Oh, it's fine—newly painted and standing in your yard.

MAUDINE. Richard, your pink flamingo is back!

RICHARD. Oh, goody-goody.

MAVIS. But, Charlie, why did you do all that?

OFFICER. There's a reason. Go ahead, Charlie. Tell 'em why you did it.

CHARLIE. It was our Christmas present to the neighborhood.

(*Everyone looks at each other, puzzled.*)

BERNIE. We don't understand.

CHARLIE. It's our way of thanking all of you for helping us out at a time when we really needed it.

SUE. A few years ago when Sally was very sick and needed medicine, and Charlie was out of work, all of you came to our rescue. You brought food, clothing, and everything we needed when we were desperate. We were so thankful.

CHARLIE. Bernie, you gave me a job at your store. Remember? I've never forgotten that!

EDDIE. When we moved here and started visiting with you, Dad saw our chance to do something nice for you.

SALLY. And it was fun doing it secretly. You know, like the Bible says, don't let your left hand know what your right hand is doing. (*She holds up the wrong hands as she speaks, and Eddie gives her a questioning look.*) Well, it does!

CHARLIE. We hope you'll forgive us for making you worry. We had planned to return all the things before you noticed they were missing. (*Turns to officer.*) Can we go home now, or are you taking us to jail?

AUNT VERA. No, indeed, he's not taking you to jail! You were only doing what Jesus taught: *Love your neighbors as yourself.* You're going to the Christmas program with all of us, your neighbors. (*Looks at everyone else.*) Right?

ALL. Right!

FLOSSIE. Before we go, do we have time for Bernie to read the Christmas story from Grandpa's Bible?

PASTOR. Yes, I think so. Bernie. (*Everyone gets settled as Bernie opens the Bible.*)

(*Curtain closes.*)

Scene 6

Nativity

(*Curtain opens with Joseph, Mary, and baby Jesus on center stage. Narrator reads all scripture from offstage.*)

NARRATOR, *reading Luke 2:1–7.* And it came to pass in those days, that there went out a decree from Caesar Augustus, that all the world should be taxed. (And this taxing was first made when Cyrenius was governor of Syria.) And all went to be taxed, every one into his own city. And Joseph also went up from Galilee, out of the city of Nazareth, into Judaea, unto the city of David, which is called Bethlehem; (because he was of the house and lineage of David:) To be taxed with Mary his espoused wife, being great with child. And so it was, that, while they were there, the days were accomplished that she should be delivered. And she brought forth her firstborn son, and wrapped him in swaddling clothes, and laid him in a manger; because there was no room for them in the inn.

("What Child Is This?" is played or sung.)

NARRATOR, *reading Luke 2:8.* And there were in the same country shepherds abiding in the field, keeping watch over their flock by night.

(Shepherds walk up aisle toward stage; they huddle at front, just off stage right.)

NARRATOR, *reading Luke 2:9–12.* And, lo, the angel of the Lord came upon them, and the glory of the Lord shone round about them: and they were sore afraid. And the angel said unto them, Fear not: for, behold, I bring you good tidings of great joy, which shall be to all people. For unto you is born this day in the city of David a Saviour, which is Christ the Lord. And this shall be a sign unto you; Ye shall find the babe wrapped in swaddling clothes, lying in a manger.

(An angel appears to the shepherds, who are frightened.)

NARRATOR, *reading Luke 2:13–14.* And suddenly there was with the angel a multitude of the heavenly host praising God, and saying, Glory to God in the highest, and on earth peace, good will toward men.

(A multitude of angels join first angel.)

NARRATOR, *reading Luke 2:15.* And it came to pass, as the angels were gone away from them into heaven, the shepherds said one to another, Let us now go even unto Bethlehem, and see this thing which is come to pass, which the Lord hath made known unto us.

(*Angels stand behind Mary, Joseph, and Jesus at back center stage.*)

NARRATOR, *reading Luke 2:16.* And they came with haste, and found Mary, and Joseph, and the babe lying in a manger.

Shepherds quickly enter stage right, beside the manger.

NARRATOR, *reading Matthew 2:1–2.* Now when Jesus was born in Bethlehem of Judaea in the days of Herod the king, behold, there came wise men from the east to Jerusalem, Saying, Where is he that is born King of the Jews? for we have seen his star in the east, and are come to worship him.

(*As song "We Three Kings" is played, the wise men come slowly up aisle toward stage, stopping at stage left, beside the manger. Each carries a gift.*)

NARRATOR, *reading Matthew 2:11.* And when they were come into the house, they saw the young child with Mary his mother, and fell down, and worshipped him: and when they had opened their treasures, they presented unto him gifts; gold, and frankincense, and myrrh.

(*Wise men kneel one at a time, present gifts to Jesus, and then stand.*)

NARRATOR, *reading John 3:16–17.* For God so loved the world, that he gave his only begotten Son, that whosoever believeth on him should not perish, but have everlasting life. For God sent not his Son into the world to condemn the world; but that the world through him might be saved.

(*"O Holy Night" is sung as solo. Curtain closes.*)

(*John and Amelia step out from behind curtain, stage left, and face audience.*)

AMELIA. I think the program gets better every year, don't you, John?

JOHN. Uh-huh.

AMELIA. And this business about the missing things—who would ever have imagined it would end like it did? (*Pauses, then looks directly at John.*) Yes, I know, you had it all figured out. You tried to tell them, but no one would listen. They probably didn't understand you. You do get so excited when you start talking. Oh, well, let's go home, okay?

JOHN. Uh-huh!

(*They exit down aisle as Richard and Maudine step out from behind curtain.*)

RICHARD. Well, Maudine, you did it again, didn't you? Jumped to conclusions before you heard all the facts.

MAUDINE. I'm sorry, Richard. I know what you mean. But I've already apologized to Lydia for thinking she might have known something about the missing things. She's forgiven me, and we're friends again.

RICHARD. Well, good!

MAUDINE. *sweetly.* Oh, Richard, guess what I got you for Christmas.

RICHARD. Earmuffs?

MAUDINE, *chuckling.* Dear, be serious. It's something that I never knew you liked so much until all this happened. (*They start down the aisle.*)

RICHARD, *suddenly realizes what she's saying, shakes his head.* Oh, please, no, no, no!

MAUDINE. I'll give you a clue. It's standing in our yard.

RICHARD, *shaking his head as he goes out the door.* No, no, no!

MAUDINE. It's *pink*!

RICHARD, *loudly and emphatically, from outside door.* No, no, no!

End

Sonny Needs a Rest

Characters

Sonny
Lucy
Mac
Charlene
Lorna
Jane
Grandma
Pastor
Grandpa
Lucas
George
Narrator
Betty
Joe
Marie
Wanda
Irene
Edward
Mary
Joseph
Shepherds
Angels
Wise men

Scene 1

NARRATOR. *Speaking in front of closed curtain to the audience.* Sonny is a famous Nashville musician. Originally from the little town of Procious, West Virginia, he hasn't been back for many years. His grandparents raised him and are very proud of him. Lately, he's gotten tired of all the tours and TV appearances. He needs a rest.

(*Curtain opens on Sonny's studio in Nashville. Sonny has a guitar on his lap; he plays slowly for a few seconds; then stops and stares out into space. His agents, Mac and Lorna, come rushing in excitedly.*)

MAC. Sonny, wait 'til you hear this!

LORNA. Yeah, just wait 'til you hear this!

SONNY, *looking disinterested.* What?

MAC. You'll never believe it!

LORNA. Never! You'll never believe it!

SONNY. What are you talking about?

MAC. Well, I'll tell you, but you'll never believe it. You are going to perform at Radison Square Garden in *New York City*!

LORNA. Yeah! The one in New York! You don't believe it, do you?

MAC. And that's not all! Get this—Reva McIntosh wants you to do a TV special with her when we can work it out. Sometime soon!

LORNA. Yeah! Sometime soon!

SONNY. Okay.

MAC. What's wrong with you? This is big news! All you can say is "okay"?

SONNY. I'm sorry. It *is* big news, and I appreciate all you've done—both of you. I'm just tired. I need a rest. It's almost Christmas, and I haven't seen my family in a long time. (*Lays guitar down.*) I'm going home for a rest. (*Exits stage, leaving Mac and Lorna shrugging in disbelief.*)

(*Curtain closes.*)

Scene 2

(*Curtain opens on Grandma and Grandpa's house. Sonny is asleep on the couch. Grandma and Grandpa are sitting in chairs.*)

GRANDMA. It's so good to see Sonny again. He's not been home for a long time.

GRANDPA. I know. It's been several years. But you have to remember he's famous now and real busy. Why, he travels all over the world a-pickin' and a-grinnin'. We can't expect him to stop by here too often.

GRANDMA. Of course you're right, dear. And he *does* call often and keep in touch.

GRANDPA. I'm just glad he's here now. Maybe he can help us out with the Christmas program at the church.

GRANDMA. Wouldn't that be great? He used to love being in the programs. He always played Joseph, you know. (*Starts laughing.*)

GRANDPA. What's so funny about playing Joseph?

GRANDMA, *still laughing.* I was just remembering the time we had live animals in the Nativity scene, and the sheep kept trying to eat Joseph's beard.

GRANDPA. Oh, yes. That *was* funny! (*Both laugh loudly.*)

SONNY, *waking; sitting up and stretching.* What's going on, Grandma?

GRANDMA. Oh, I'm sorry, Sonny. We woke you up. Go back to sleep. We'll be quiet.

SONNY. That's okay. What were you laughing about?

GRANDPA. We were thinking back to that Christmas program we had years ago when we had the live animals, and—

SONNY, *interrupting.* And the sheep kept eating my beard. I had forgotten about that. We used to have a lot of fun putting on those programs, didn't we?

GRANDMA. We sure did! (*Nudges Grandpa.*) Since you're here, Sonny, maybe you'd like to help us out with this year's program.

GRANDPA. Say, that's a great idea! We need all the help we can get.

SONNY. Nah, Grandpa, I outgrew all that a long time ago. Christmas is just a holiday I don't have time for anymore. Besides, I'm here to rest, remember? So you celebrate Christmas your way, and I'll celebrate Christmas my way. (*Lies down.*)

(*Curtain closes.*)

Scene 3

(*Curtain opens on committee meeting at Grandma and Grandpa's house. Committee members are gathered on stage left.*)

GEORGE. I don't know how we're going to do it.

BETTY. What do you mean? Do what?

(*Door opens; Sonny walks in.*)

SONNY. Oh, I'm sorry, Grandma. I didn't know you had company. I'll come back later. (*Turns to leave*)

GRANDPA. No, don't leave, Sonny. This is our Christmas Outreach Committee from the church. This is Betty.

BETTY, *swooning and very impressed.* Oh, I saw you on TV last week.

GRANDPA. This is Irene and her sister, Wanda. (*They shake hands with Sonny*)

WANDA. I've seen *all* your movies.

SONNY. Oh, well, okay.

IRENE, *to Wanda.* Why on earth did you say that?

WANDA. What?

IRENE. He doesn't make movies. He's a musician.

WANDA. Well, when he makes a movie, I'll go see it!

(*Irene rolls eyes in disbelief.*)

GRANDPA. This is George.

GEORGE. Hello, Sonny. You know, I used to play accordion back in my younger days. I was pretty good at it, too. You just holler when you need me.

SONNY. I'll do that. Thanks.

GRANDPA. This is Joe.

SONNY. Hi, Joe. You doing okay?

JOE. Uh-huh!

GRANDPA. And this is Marie.

MARIE. Hi, Sonny. I guess people like you are always looking for new talent, aren't you? I did a song at church last week. It goes like this. (*Begins singing off key.*)

SONNY. *Quickly interrupting Marie's song.* I'd better not interrupt your meeting now. We'll talk about it later.

GEORGE. I know your grandma and grandpa are glad you're here to help out with the Christmas program, Sonny.

GRANDMA. No, Sonny's not helping with the Christmas program. Sonny's here for a rest.

SONNY. You go ahead with your meeting. I'll just sit over here.

BETTY. George, what did you mean when you said you didn't know how we're going to do it? Do what?

GEORGE. We cannot buy toys and food for the needy like we did last year. We don't have the money.

GRANDMA. But they count on us to help them. There's got to be some way!

GEORGE. Well, we'll do the best we can. But right now I just don't think there's any way.

MARIE. If we can't come up with the money, then maybe we'll just have to forget it for this year.

GRANDPA. I say, God will provide. He always has, and he always will. Right, Joe?

JOE. Uh-huh!

(*Sonny rubs his chin while pondering what he has heard.*)

(*Curtain closes.*)

Scene 4

(*Curtain opens on Grandma and Grandpa's house. Sonny is asleep on the couch. Members of another committee are gathered at stage left.*)

EDWARD, *standing.* I now call the Scenery and Props Committee to order. (*Slams hand on table.*)

SONNY, *sitting up quickly.* What on earth?

GRANDMA. Oh, Sonny, we woke you up again. I'm sorry. You go back to sleep. We'll be quiet.

SONNY. That's all right. Another committee meeting?

GRANDPA. Yes, this is the Scenery and Props Committee. This is Jane, Lucy, Charlene, and Edward. (*Addresses committee members.*) Sonny is here for a rest.

EDWARD, *handing a paper to Sonny.* I have something for you. Here.

SONNY. What's this?

EDWARD. It's a song I wrote. I figured you are always looking for new material.

SONNY. Thank you. I'll keep it in mind. (*Folds the paper.*)

EDWARD. I could sing it for you.

LUCY, *looking at her watch and shaking her head.* Oh, is that the time already?

CHARLENE, *also looking at her watch and shaking her head.* I've gotta go pretty soon.

JANE, *looking at her watch and shaking her head.* I have to go feed the chickens.

EDWARD. You don't have chickens.

JANE. Well, then, I have to feed the cows. There must be something I have to feed.

SONNY. Maybe you'd better go ahead with your meeting. We'll talk later, Edward.

JANE. Well, first of all, we need some new scenery. What we used last year got wet, and it's ruined.

CHARLENE. Our costumes are worn out, too.

LUCY. Yeah, we could make new ones if we had the material.

EDWARD. That's the trouble. We don't have money for any of that. The new roof took everything we had.

JANE. Say! Maybe Sonny could help us. How about it, Sonny? Any idea how we could raise some money?

SONNY, *getting up.* Well, I know some people. Maybe I could talk to them and see.

GRANDPA, *guiding Sonny back to couch.* No! I told you Sonny is here for a rest. (*Sits down.*) I say God will provide. He always has, and he always will!

(*Phone rings. Grandma answers.*)

GRANDMA. Hello. Oh, no, that's terrible! (*Pauses.*) That's awful! (*Pauses.*) Oh, that's terrible! (*Pauses.*) That's awful! (*Pauses.*) Okay, bye.

EVERYBODY. What? What?

GRANDMA. Something terrible's happened!

EVERYBODY. What? What?

GRANDMA. The pastor said Charlie Morton broke his leg, and he won't be able to walk on it for several weeks.

LUCY. Oh, that *is* terrible. And he's our music director! What else is going to happen?

CHARLENE. Well, that is the last straw! We can't have a Christmas program without music.

(*They all bow their heads in despair and sit in silence.*)

SONNY. Hey, don't give up so soon. There must be a way out of this. Maybe I can help after all.

GRANDPA. Now, Sonny, we don't want to burden you with our problems. You're here to rest.

SONNY. Hold on! I'll get my rest. I've been listening to all of you, and I'm getting back to what Christmas is all about. It's about using what we have to help others. I remember from Sunday school that's what

Jesus taught. I'll talk to some people. You'll have the money you need, and I'll see what I can do about the music. Okay?

(*As everyone rushes to thank Sonny, there's a knock at door.*)

GRANDMA, *answering*. Well, come in, Pastor. You too, Lucas.

PASTOR. Sonny, I know you're here to rest, but we really need your help. We don't have any music for the Christmas program,

LUCAS. And we'll have to cancel if we can't find any. You're our last hope, Sonny.

PASTOR. What do you say? Will you please help us out?

SONNY. Yes, I'd be happy to.

PASTOR, *pleased and surprised*. Well, I didn't think it would be that easy!

(*Everyone laughs.*)

(*Curtain closes.*)

Scene 5

Nativity

(*Curtain opens with Joseph, Mary, and baby Jesus on center stage. Narrator reads all scripture from offstage.*)

NARRATOR, *reading Luke 2:1–7*. And it came to pass in those days, that there went out a decree from Caesar Augustus, that all the world should be taxed. (And this taxing was first made when Cyrenius was governor of Syria.) And all went to be taxed, every one into his own city. And Joseph also went up from Galilee, out of the city of Nazareth, into Judaea, unto the city of David, which is called

Bethlehem; (because he was of the house and lineage of David:) To be taxed with Mary his espoused wife, being great with child. And so it was, that, while they were there, the days were accomplished that she should be delivered. And she brought forth her firstborn son, and wrapped him in swaddling clothes, and laid him in a manger; because there was no room for them in the inn.

(*"What Child Is This?" is played or sung.*)

NARRATOR, *reading Luke 2:8.* And there were in the same country shepherds abiding in the field, keeping watch over their flock by night.

(*Shepherds walk up aisle toward stage; they huddle at front, just off stage right.*)

NARRATOR, *reading Luke 2:9–12.* And, lo, the angel of the Lord came upon them, and the glory of the Lord shone round about them: and they were sore afraid. And the angel said unto them, Fear not: for, behold, I bring you good tidings of great joy, which shall be to all people. For unto you is born this day in the city of David a Saviour, which is Christ the Lord. And this shall be a sign unto you; Ye shall find the babe wrapped in swaddling clothes, lying in a manger.

(*An angel appears to the shepherds, who are frightened.*)

NARRATOR, *reading Luke 2:13–14.* And suddenly there was with the angel a multitude of the heavenly host praising God, and saying, Glory to God in the highest, and on earth peace, good will toward men.

(*A multitude of angels join first angel.*)

NARRATOR, *reading Luke 2:15.* And it came to pass, as the angels were gone away from them into heaven, the shepherds said one to another, Let us now go even unto Bethlehem, and see this thing which is come to pass, which the Lord hath made known unto us.

(*Angels stand behind Mary, Joseph, and Jesus at back center stage.*)

NARRATOR, *reading Luke 2:16.* And they came with haste, and found Mary, and Joseph, and the babe lying in a manger.

(*Shepherds quickly enter stage right, beside the manger.*)

NARRATOR, *reading Matthew 2:1–2.* Now when Jesus was born in Bethlehem of Judaea in the days of Herod the king, behold, there came wise men from the east to Jerusalem, Saying, Where is he that is born King of the Jews? for we have seen his star in the east, and are come to worship him.

(*As song "We Three Kings" is played, the wise men come slowly up aisle toward stage, stopping at stage left, beside the manger. Each carries a gift.*)

NARRATOR, *reading Matthew 2:11.* And when they were come into the house, they saw the young child with Mary his mother, and fell down, and worshipped him: and when they had opened their treasures, they presented unto him gifts; gold, and frankincense, and myrrh.

(*Wise men kneel one at a time, present gifts to Jesus, and then stand.*)

NARRATOR, *reading John 3:16–17.* For God so loved the world, that he gave his only begotten Son, that whosoever believeth on him should not perish, but have everlasting life. For God sent not his Son into the world to condemn the world; but that the world through him might be saved.

(*"O Holy Night" is sung as solo.*)

End

Good Tidings of Great Joy

Characters

Zacharias

Gabriel

Mary

Elisabeth

Joseph

Innkeeper

Innkeeper's Wife

Herod

Herod's Wife

Chief Priest

Wise Men

Scribe

Angel 1

Angel 2

Angel 3

Angel 4

Angela

Shepherd 1

Shepherd 2

Shepherd 3

Narrator

Scene 1

Angel talks to Zacharias

NARRATOR, *reading Matthew 11:10–11 from behind closed curtain.* "For this is he of whom it is written, Behold I send my messenger before thy face, which shall prepare thy way before thee. Verily I say unto you, Among them that are born of women there hath not risen a greater than John the Baptist: not withstanding he that is least in the kingdom of heaven is greater than he."

(*Zacharias is kneeling in prayer as curtain opens.*)

GABRIEL, *entering.* Your prayer has been heard, Zacharias.

ZACHARIAS, *rising, fearful.* Who are you? How did you get in here?

GABRIEL. Don't be afraid, Zacharias, God has heard your prayer. Your wife, Elisabeth, will have a son, and you will call his name John. He will be great in God's eyes. Even before he is born, he will be filled with the Holy Spirit. He will prepare the people for the coming of the Lord Jesus.

ZACHARIAS. Are you sure about this? I am an old man, and Elisabeth is too old to have a child. Surely what you are saying cannot happen.

GABRIEL. I am Gabriel. I stand in God's presence, and I have been sent to tell you this good news. Now, because you haven't believed what I have told you, you won't be able to speak again until all these things have come to pass.

(*Gabriel slowly moves offstage. Zacharias turns to face audience, stares out, and puts fingers to lips.*)

(*Curtain closes.*)

Scene 2

Angel talks to Mary

NARRATOR, *reading Isaiah 7.14 from behind closed curtain.* "Therefore the Lord himself shall give you a sign; Behold, a virgin shall conceive, and bear a son, and shall call his name Immanuel."

(*Mary mixes something in a bowl in her house as the curtain opens.*)

GABRIEL, *entering.* Mary.

MARY. Hello. Do I know you?

GABRIEL. I am the angel Gabriel, sent from God to tell you that the Lord is with you. You are highly favored and blessed among women.

MARY, *hand going to chest in shock*. What do you mean? I don't understand.

GABRIEL. Don't be afraid, Mary. God has chosen you to bear his son, and you shall call him Jesus. He will be great and shall be called the Son of the Highest. God will give unto him the throne of his father, David. He will rule over the house of Jacob forever, and there shall be no end to his kingdom.

MARY. But I have no husband. How can this be?

GABRIEL. The Holy Spirit will come upon you, and the Spirit of the Most High will overshadow you. The child will be called holy, the Son of God. Your cousin Elisabeth is also going to have a child.

MARY, *showing surprise*. But she is barren and beyond childbearing age.

GABRIEL. This is the sixth month with her. With God, nothing is impossible.

MARY, *bowing*). I am the Lord's servant. Whatever he says, I accept.

(*Gabriel backs offstage.*)

(*Curtain closes.*)

Scene 3

Angel talks to Joseph

NARRATOR, *reading Matthew 1.18 behind closed curtain*. "Now the birth of Jesus Christ was on this wise. When as his mother Mary was espoused to Joseph, before they came together, she was found with child of the Holy Ghost."

(*As curtain opens, Joseph is alone on stage, pacing; he is sad and troubled. A bed is on stage.*)

JOSEPH. What am I going to do? Mary and I are to be married. Now I find out she is going to have a child. How could she do this to me? She has deceived me. But I can't help myself. I still love her, and I don't want to embarrass her. I'll have to send her away privately. (*Cries out in despair.*) Oh, Mary! (*He lies down to sleep.*)

GABRIEL, *entering.* Joseph, do not be afraid to take Mary as your wife. She has not deceived you. The child she is going to have is of the Holy Ghost. She will have a son, and you will call him Jesus, for he will save his people from their sins. (*Slowly backs offstage.*)

(*Joseph sits up and curiously looks around. Curtain closes.*)

Scene 4

Mary visits Elisabeth

NARRATOR, *reading Luke 1.39–40 from behind closed curtain.* "And Mary arose in those days, and went into the hill country with haste, into a city of Juda; And entered into the house of Zacharias, and saluted Elisabeth."

(*Curtain opens. Elisabeth is sitting in her chair. Mary opens door and looks in.*)

MARY. Elisabeth, are you there?

ELISABETH, *rising slowly, she stops quickly as she feels her baby move inside her. She puts her hand on her abdomen and smiles. Mary, is* that you? Oh, how good to see you! (*She embraces Mary.*) You are with child, aren't you?

MARY. How did you know?

ELISABETH. When I heard your voice, my baby leaped with joy. I am so glad you have come to see me. You are blessed among all women.

MARY. Oh, Elisabeth, I do truly praise God. I don't know why I should be so blessed to bear the Son of God, but I believe God is working miracles through us.

ELISABETH. How does Joseph feel about all this?

MARY. An angel appeared to him also and told him what was going to be. He knows it is God's doing. He accepts it. We must trust God to lead us.

ELISABETH. Yes, Mary, you're right. Now you must be tired from your journey. You must rest. (*Both start to exit stage; then stop.*) I just thought of something. Some day our little boys may play together. (*They exit stage; curtain closes.*)

Scene 5

Angels in Heaven

NARRATOR, *reading Psalm 103:20 behind closed curtain.* "Bless the Lord, ye his angels, that excel in strength, that do his commandments, hearkening unto the voice of his word."

(*Curtain opens. Angels 1,2,3, and 4 are walking around excitedly.*)

ANGEL 1. Can't you feel it? Can't you *just* feel it?

ANGEL 2. What?

ANGEL 1. The excitement! Can't you feel the excitement in the air?

ANGEL 3. I can! I can feel it! Something *big* is about to happen.

ANGEL 4. What do you think it is?

ANGEL 3. I have no idea. But with all the activity going on, it has to be *big*—maybe the *biggest* thing that's ever happened!

ANGEL 1. Even bigger than the creation?

ANGEL 3. I don't know, but it's *big*!

ANGEL 4. Even bigger than the flood?

ANGEL 3. I told you, I don't know!

ANGEL 2. Do you think *He* will have a job for us?

ANGEL 3. We'll find out soon. He called for Angela. As soon as she gets back, we'll find out what's going on. (*Looks toward Angela as she enters.*) Here she comes now.

ANGEL 4, *to Angela.* Did you see him? What's going on?

ANGEL 1. Yeah! What's going on?

ANGELA. He wants me to take a message tonight to some shepherds on a hillside.

ANGEL 3. *whining.* You got to take the *last* message. I think it's my turn.

ANGEL 2, *to Angel 3.* Shhh! (*Turns to Angela.*) What is the message?

ANGELA. Tonight in Bethlehem, Jesus, the Son of God, will be born.

(*All are surprised and joyful.*)

ANGEL 1. Can we go with you? Please let us go with you!

ANGELA. We're all going! Let's go get ready. We've got a big night ahead of us.

ANGEL 3, *to Angel 2 as they exit.* See, I told you it was *big*!

(Curtain closes.)

Scene 6

Shepherds on Hillside

NARRATOR, *reading Luke 2:8 from behind closed curtain.* "And there were in the same country shepherds abiding in the field, keeping watch over their flock by night."

(*Shepherds begin talking as they proceed down aisle toward closed curtain. They stop in front of curtain.*)

SHEPHERD 1. The sky looks different tonight. There's a strange glow in it.

SHEPHERD 2, *looking up.* I know what you mean. It does look different. Do you think it's going to storm?

SHEPHERD 1. Nah. It doesn't have the look of a storm, does it?

SHEPHERD 3. Huh-uh!

SHEPHERD 2. Did you notice how quiet the sheep are? Most of the time they're so noisy we can't hear each other talk.

SHEPHERD 1. It's like they sense danger or know that something is about to happen.

SHEPHERD 2, *mockingly.* What's going to happen? Tonight is like every other night. We tend our sheep and lambs and make sure they're safe. Right?

SHEPHERD 3. Uh-huh!

SHEPHERD 1. Well, I know one thing's the same as every other night—it's cold out here! Let's build a fire and get warm.

(*Curtain opens to reveal Angela and other angels on center stage. Shepherds react in fear.*)

ANGELA. Fear not: for behold, I bring you good tidings of great joy, which shall be to all people. For unto you is born this day in the city of David a Savior, which is Christ the Lord. And this shall be a sign unto you; Ye shall find the babe wrapped in swaddling clothes, lying in a manger.

ANGELS. *with arms reaching up.* Glory to God in the highest, and on earth peace, good will toward men. (*Curtain closes.*)

SHEPHERD 1. Did you hear that?

SHEPHERD 2. Yes! We have to go to Bethlehem now to see what they were talking about. I knew there was something special about this night.

SHEPHERD 1. What about the sheep? What are we going to do with them?

SHEPHERD 2. Do *you* want to stay and look after them?

SHEPHERD 1. Not me! (*Turns to Shepherd 3.*) Do *you*?

SHEPHERD 3. Huh-uh!

SHEPHERD 1. Then let's all go to Bethlehem!

(*They exit hurriedly back the way they came in.*)

Scene 7

Innkeeper and Wife

NARRATOR, *reading Matthew 8:20 behind closed curtain.* "And Jesus saith unto him, The foxes have holes, and the birds of the air have nests; but the Son of man hath not where to lay his head."

(*Curtain opens, with innkeeper seated at table, counting money.*)

WIFE, *rushing in excitedly.* Husband, you'll never believe!

HUSBAND. Shhh! (*Continues counting, then looks at her.*) Now, what is it?

WIFE. Remember that nice young couple that stopped yesterday and wanted a room?

HUSBAND. Don't start that again! I told you, just like I told them. We didn't have a room. It's been a crazy, busy time with the census and all. Not that I'm complaining. (*Smiles as he holds up bag of money.*)

WIFE. I felt so sorry for them. You know she was expecting a baby.

HUSBAND. I know that. But I couldn't put someone else out just so they could have a room, could I? I felt sorry for them too. That's why I let them stay in the stable. It's the only place I had. (*Stops abruptly.*) Wait a minute. What do you mean, she *was* expecting a baby?

WIFE, *excitedly.* Oh, that's what I came to tell you! She had her baby last night in the stable.

HUSBAND. Last night? In the stable? Is she okay? Is the baby all right?

WIFE. Yes, yes, yes, and yes. It's a beautiful little boy, and they're all fine. Help me gather up some things they need, and we'll take them out to them. (*Frantically looks around.*)

HUSBAND, *taking her by the shoulders.* Calm down, wife. Babies are born every day.

WIFE. But this one was born in a stable. (*Turns to face audience.*) And I have a feeling this is a very special baby. (*Looks at husband.*) Now, come on. Help me. (*They exit quickly.*)

(*Curtain closes.*)

Scene 8

King Herod

NARRATOR, *reading Matthew 2:3 from behind closed curtain.* "When Herod the king had heard these things, he was troubled, and all Jerusalem with him."

(*Curtain opens, with Herod and wife on stage.*)

MRS. HEROD, *relaxing on couch, while the king paces back and forth.* My king, what is wrong? I have never seen you like this. Are you ill?

HEROD. No! I am not ill! I have heard rumors—disturbing rumors!

MRS. HEROD. Rumors? What rumors? Rumors cannot hurt you. You are the king!

HEROD. I hear talk that another king has been born—a King of the Jews! I have sent for the chief priest and scribe to tell me more of this. Ah, here they come now. (*Shouts.*) Enter!

(*Chief priest and scribe enter and bow to king.*)

CHIEF PRIEST. Your Royal Majesty. What do you desire?

HEROD. I *desire* to know where this new king is to be born. Wise men from the East have come looking for him. (*Tone becomes mocking.*) To worship him. (*Becomes angry.*) I am king. I will not share my throne! Where is this "king" to be born? You are supposed to know these things. Tell me!

SCRIBE. It is written by the prophet, "Out of Bethlehem shall come a Governor, which shall rule my people Israel."

HEROD. Bethlehem, huh? I will see these wise men again. I will tell them to go find the young child and then come back to tell me where he is. (*Speaks facetiously to audience.*) After all, I will want to go to worship him also. (*To priest and scribe.*) Now, *go!*

(Curtain closes.)

Scene 9

Nativity

(*Curtain opens with Joseph, Mary, and baby Jesus on center stage. Narrator reads all scripture from offstage.*)

NARRATOR, *reading Luke 2:1–7.* And it came to pass in those days, that there went out a decree from Caesar Augustus, that all the world should be taxed. (And this taxing was first made when Cyrenius was governor of Syria.) And all went to be taxed, every one into his own city. And Joseph also went up from Galilee, out of the city of Nazareth, into Judaea, unto the city of David, which is called Bethlehem; (because he was of the house and lineage of David:) To be taxed with Mary his espoused wife, being great with child. And so it was, that, while they were there, the days were accomplished that she should be delivered. And she brought forth her firstborn son, and wrapped him in swaddling clothes, and laid him in a manger; because there was no room for them in the inn.

("What Child Is This?" is played or sung.)

NARRATOR, *reading Luke 2:8.* And there were in the same country shepherds abiding in the field, keeping watch over their flock by night.

(Shepherds walk up aisle toward stage; they huddle at front, just off stage right.

NARRATOR, *reading Luke 2:9–12.* And, lo, the angel of the Lord came upon them, and the glory of the Lord shone round about them: and they were sore afraid. And the angel said unto them, Fear not: for, behold, I bring you good tidings of great joy, which shall be to all people. For unto you is born this day in the city of David a Saviour, which is Christ the Lord. And this shall be a sign unto you; Ye shall find the babe wrapped in swaddling clothes, lying in a manger.

(An angel appears to the shepherds, who are frightened.)

NARRATOR, *reading Luke 2:13–14.* And suddenly there was with the angel a multitude of the heavenly host praising God, and saying, Glory to God in the highest, and on earth peace, good will toward men.

(A multitude of angels join first angel.)

NARRATOR, *reading Luke 2:15.* And it came to pass, as the angels were gone away from them into heaven, the shepherds said one to another, Let us now go even unto Bethlehem, and see this thing which is come to pass, which the Lord hath made known unto us.

(*Angels stand behind Mary, Joseph, and Jesus at back center stage.*)

NARRATOR, *reading Luke 2:16.* And they came with haste, and found Mary, and Joseph, and the babe lying in a manger.

(*Shepherds quickly enter stage right, beside the manger.*)

NARRATOR, *reading Matthew 2:1–2.* Now when Jesus was born in Bethlehem of Judaea in the days of Herod the king, behold, there came wise men from the east to Jerusalem, Saying, Where is he that is born King of the Jews? for we have seen his star in the east, and are come to worship him.

(*As song "We Three Kings" is played, the wise men come slowly up aisle toward stage, stopping at stage left, beside the manger. Each carries a gift.*)

NARRATOR, *reading Matthew 2:11.* And when they were come into the house, they saw the young child with Mary his mother, and fell down, and worshipped him: and when they had opened their treasures, they presented unto him gifts; gold, and frankincense, and myrrh.

(*Wise men kneel one at a time, present gifts to Jesus, and then stand.*)

NARRATOR, *reading John 3:16–17.* For God so loved the world, that he gave his only begotten Son, that whosoever believeth on him should not perish, but have everlasting life. For God sent not his Son into the world to condemn the world; but that the world through him might be saved.

(*"O Holy Night" is sung as solo.*)

End

Jesus, Master of Metaphors

Characters

Narrator
Elijah
Adrianne

(*Curtain opens. Elijah and Adrianne are on stage.*)

NARRATOR. *To audience from stage right.* Jesus was the master of metaphors. His disciples asked Him why He spoke to the people in parables. He told them it was given unto them, the disciples, to know the mysteries of the kingdom of heaven, but to the others it was not given. Through speaking of things they could relate to, maybe they would understand what the kingdom of heaven was like. We will now feature eight of these parables.

1. The Wheat and the Tares

ELIJAH. "The kingdom of heaven is likened unto a man which sowed good seed in his field."

ADRIANNE. Hey, that's a nice patch of wheat you have there.

ELIJAH. Thanks, I try to take care of it and do everything I can to make it grow.

ADRIANNE. Uh-oh! I think I see some nasty-looking weeds growing in there too.

ELIJAH. Oh, I know. As hard as I try, I can't seem to keep the weeds out.

ADRIANNE. Well, that's no problem! I'm a pretty good weed-puller. (*Pulls up sleeves.*) I can yank those weeds out in no time.

ELIJAH. No! No! We can't do that! If we pull up the weeds, we'll pull up the good wheat too. We'll let them grow together. Then at harvest, we'll separate them. We'll burn the weeds and gather the wheat in the barn.

NARRATOR, *reading Matthew 13:37–43.* "He answered and said unto them, He that soweth the good seed is the Son of man; The field is the world; the good seed are the children of the kingdom; but the tares are the children of the wicked one; The enemy that sowed them is the devil; the harvest is the end of the world; and reapers are the angels. As therefore the tares are gathered and burned in the fire; so shall it be in the end of this world. The Son of man shall send forth his angels, and they shall gather out of his kingdom all things that offend, and them which do iniquity; And shall cast them into a furnace of fire: there shall be wailing and gnashing of teeth. Then shall the righteous shine forth as the sun in the kingdom of their Father. Who hath ears to hear, let him hear."

2. The Mustard Seed

ADRIANNE. "The kingdom of heaven is like to a grain of mustard seed, which a man took, and sowed in his field."

ELIJAH. Whatcha got there?

ADRIANNE. It's a grain of mustard seed.

ELIJAH. Where? I don't see it.

ADRIANNE. There! See? Right there!

ELIJAH. Oh, yeah. I see it now. Whatcha gonna do with it?

ADRIANNE. I'm gonna plant it!

ELIJAH. You're gonna plant it? You're kidding! Something that small won't grow.

ADRIANNE. We'll see. (*Both walk offstage.*)

NARRATOR. Sometime later. (*Elijah and Adrianne return to stage.*)

ELIJAH. Hey, what about that grain of mustard seed you planted? Didn't do anything, did it?

ADRIANNE. That's it, right over there. (*Points yonder.*)

ELIJAH. Where? I can't see anything for that big tree.

ADRIANNE. That's it! That big tree that all the birds are lodging in.

ELIJAH. Really? Well, I guess that shows that something very small can produce *big* results! (*Both leave stage.*)

NARRATOR, *reading Mark 4:30–32.* "And he said, Whereunto shall we liken the kingdom of God? or with what comparison shall we compare it? It is like a grain of mustard seed, which, when it is sown in the earth, is less that all the seeds that be in the earth: But when it is sown, it groweth up, and becometh greater than all herbs, and shooteth out great branches; so that the fowls of the air may lodge under the shadow of it."

3. The Wedding Garment

ELIJAH. "The Kingdom of Heaven is like unto a certain king, which made a marriage for his son."

ADRIANNE. There would be a lot of people at *that* wedding.

ELIJAH. Well, you would think so. But I heard that he sent his servants to tell the guests it was time, and they wouldn't come.

ADRIANNE. Why not?

ELIJAH. I don't know. They made all kinds of excuses. Said they had other things to do. And I heard there was lots of good food there, too.

ADRIANNE. What did they do? Call off the wedding?

ELIJAH. No, the king sent his servants out to invite people off the streets. And, of course, *they* came! After all, they were gonna get a good meal.

ADRIANNE. So everything turned out okay, huh?

ELIJAH. Not quite. When the king came in, he saw a man who wasn't wearing a wedding garment. When the king asked him why, he didn't have an answer.

ADRIANNE. Did he get to stay anyway?

ELIJAH. No, he hadn't made himself ready for the wedding, so he couldn't go in. We all need to make sure we have on our wedding garments.

NARRATOR, *reading Revelation 19:7–8.* "Let us be glad and rejoice, and give honour to him for the marriage of the Lamb is come, and his wife hath made herself ready. And to her was granted that she should be arrayed in fine linen, clean and white; for the fine linen is the righteousness of saints." (*To audience.*) Do you have on your wedding garment?

4. Workers in the Vineyard

ADRIANNE. "For the kingdom of heaven is like unto a man that is a house-holder, which went out early in the morning to hire labourers into his vineyard."

ELIJAH. How much did you get paid?

ADRIANNE. The usual day's wage. How about you? How much did you get?

ELIJAH. The same. But it's not really fair.

ADRIANNE. What do you mean? What's not fair?

ELIJAH. All of us gettin' the same wages. We worked all day, but some of them only worked for an hour.

ADRIANNE. Yeah, we worked in the hot sun all day long, and they hardly worked up a sweat. And another thing, did you notice that we got paid last? No, this doesn't sound fair at all.

ELIJAH. I think I'm gonna talk to the boss man and find out what's going on. I don't agree with this at all. (*Starts to walk offstage.*)

ADRIANNE. Wait a minute! You said "agree." I just remembered something. When we were hired, we *agreed* to work for this wage. Didn't we?

ELIJAH. Yeah, I guess we did. You're saying we should be glad we were hired, take our wages, and not complain. Right?

ADRIANNE. Maybe so. After all, it is the boss's money, and he can do what he wants with it.

NARRATOR, *reading Matthew 20:15-16.* "Is it not lawful for me to do what I will with mine own? Is thine eye evil, because I am good? So the last shall be first, and the first last: for many be called, but few chosen."

5. Treasure in the Field

ELIJAH. "Again, the kingdom of heaven is like unto treasure hid in a field, the which when a man hath found, he hideth, and for joy thereof goeth and selleth all that he hath, and buyeth that field."

ADRIANNE. Hey, I've got to tell you something! (*Looks left, then right.*)

ELIJAH. What is it? What are you going on about?

ADRIANNE. If I don't tell somebody, I'm gonna explode!

ELIJAH. Tell me, tell me! What is it?

ADRIANNE. I was digging in that field over there (*Points left*), and I found something.

ELIJAH. Well, if you're like me, you found rocks—lots of rocks. But I don't get this excited about rocks.

ADRIANNE. Not rocks! I found a treasure!

ELIJAH. A treasure? What kind of treasure?

ADRIANNE. Oh, the greatest treasure you could ever find. I hid it, and I'm gonna go back and buy that field.

ELIJAH. How are you gonna do that? You don't have that kind of money.

ADRIANNE. I'm gonna sell all that I have and buy that field. Nothing I have could ever compare with that treasure I found.

NARRATOR, *reading Matthew 6:19–21.* "Lay not up for yourselves treasures upon earth, where moth and rust doth corrupt, and where thieves break through and steal: But lay up for yourselves treasures in heaven, where neither moth nor rust doth corrupt, and where thieves do not break through nor steal:"

6. Casting Net for Fish

ADRIANNE. "Again, the kingdom of heaven is like unto a net; that was cast into the sea, and gathered of every kind."

ELIJAH. I'm going fishin'. Wanna come? Do you like to fish?

ADRIANNE. Oh, yeah, I've caught some really big fish in my time.

ELIJAH. What kind of fishing do you like to do?

ADRIANNE. Anything that I can catch. I'm not particular.

ELIJAH. My friend and I recently went fishing together with a net. We threw it out into the water, and when we pulled it in, it was loaded with fish.

ADRIANNE. Did you have a big fish fry?

ELIJAH. Yeah, we did. But first we had to figure out what was good and what wasn't.

ADRIANNE. Did you do that all by yourself?

ELIJAH. Oh, no. I don't know that much about the different kinds of fish. But my friend does. He's really good at separating the good from the bad.

NARRATOR, *reading Matthew 13:49.* "So shall it be at the end of the world: the angels shall come forth, and sever the wicked from among the just."

7. The Talents

ADRIANNE. "For the kingdom of heaven is as a man traveling into a far country, who called his own servants, and delivered unto them his goods."

ELIJAH. I tried to tell him he should do something with his talent and not just bury it. Before the master left, he gave him one talent. But instead of doing anything with it, he hid it. He was afraid of losing it, and he ended up losing it after all.

ADRIANNE. Yeah, I feel bad for him. I knew the master wouldn't like it when he returned.

ELIJAH. He gave it to you, didn't he, to put with the five that you doubled? You did good. You used your five to gain five more.

ADRIANNE. You did too. He gave you two, and you gained two more.

ELIJAH. You know, I just thought of something. We should have put them together, and maybe we could have tripled them for the master.

ADRIANNE. No, we couldn't do that because our talents are different. The master recognized that. That's why he divided them the way he did. He knew what he was doing. He always knows what he's doing. He gives to every man according to his ability.

NARRATOR, *reading John 15:1–2.* "I AM the true vine, and my Father is the husbandman. Every branch in me that beareth not fruit he taketh away: and every branch that beareth fruit, he purgeth it, that it may bring forth more fruit."

8. Forgiveness

ELIJAH. "Therefore is the kingdom of heaven likened unto a certain king, which would take account of his servants."

ADRIANNE. Hey, I'm glad I ran into you this morning. Remember last year when I loaned you ten thousand dollars? I need it. I'm running low on funds. And you did say you'd pay me back soon.

ELIJAH. I know. I'm sorry about that. The thing is, I don't have it. I'm only working part-time, and I can't pay it back right now.

ADRIANNE. Well, I need it. I hate it, but if I have to, I'll take you to court to get what you owe me.

ELIJAH. Oh, please don't do that! My family's been sick. It's been one thing after another. If you'll give me just a little more time, I promise I'll pay it back.

ADRIANNE. I didn't know you were having so many troubles. I tell you what. Just forget about the money. You don't have to pay it back. It's okay.

ELIJAH. Oh, thank you! (*Both leave stage*).

NARRATOR, A few days later, they meet again. *(they return to stage.)*

ADRIANNE. I heard something about you yesterday that I couldn't believe.

ELIJAH. What was it?

ADRIANNE. Did you take your neighbor to court?

ELIJAH. Yes, I had to. He owed me fifty dollars, and he wouldn't pay me.

ADRIANNE. Wait a minute! What's wrong with this picture? Did you forget that I fully erased the large debt that you owed me? Now, your neighbor owes you a much smaller debt, and you threaten to take him to court. Shouldn't you have pity on him, as I had pity on you? Don't expect to be forgiven if you don't forgive.

NARRATOR, *reading Matthew 6:14–15.* "For if ye forgive men their trespasses, your heavenly Father will also forgive you: But if ye forgive not men their trespasses, neither will your Father forgive your trespasses."

End

The Prodigal Son

Characters

Interviewer
Prodigal son
Father

INTERVIEWER. Good morning and welcome to WWJD, channel 7. Today, on this Father's Day, I am interviewing the prodigal son and his father. Found in the book of Luke, this story, perhaps better than any other, shows a father's love. Please welcome the prodigal son and his father. (*Turns to son.*) Son, we'll start with you. Were you not happy at home?

SON. Well, yes, I guess I was happy enough. But I got bored. My friends were always having parties and good times. I just wasn't having any fun. Dad only gave me a small allowance, and I had to work for that.

INTERVIEWER. Is that true, sir? You made him *work* for his allowance? Why would you do that?

FATHER. I thought it might teach him responsibility. My father always told me, "If it's not worth working for, it's not worth having."

INTERVIEWER. That day, son, when you went to your father, what did you ask him?

SON. Well, I knew that someday I would get half of what my father had, but I couldn't wait for *someday*. So I told my father I wanted my inheritance, and I wanted it now.

INTERVIEWER. And, sir, how did that make you feel?

FATHER. It broke my heart, but I gave it to him, and in a few days he left.

INTERVIEWER. Where did you go?

SON. I went as far away as I could. I had big plans.

INTERVIEWER. I see. You had your freedom, you didn't have to answer to anyone, and you had all that money. I would imagine you had yourself a good time.

SON. Oh, I did. I went to a party every night. Or I had my own party. I had lots to eat, and I slept as late as I wanted to. And, I had friends with me all the time.

INTERVIEWER. Sir, were you in touch with him at all during this time?

FATHER. No, I didn't know if he was alive or dead. I just kept looking down the road, hoping and waiting for him to come home.

INTERVIEWER, *to son*. Sounds like you were living "high on the hog." You probably didn't care if you ever went home.

SON. I didn't! This was the life for me. I was doing good.

INTERVIEWER. What changed your mind?

SON. Well, first, I ran out of money. And the strangest thing—when I ran out of money, I ran out of friends. Then, to make matters worse, I got hungry.

INTERVIEWER. You mean you didn't have anything to eat? Did you think about getting a job?

SON. I got a job in the fields, feeding hogs, and I was so hungry I could have eaten the food I was giving them.

INTERVIEWER. Did you ever think of going home?

SON. At my lowest point I thought about my father's servants. They had *more* than enough to eat, and here I was, starving.

INTERVIEWER. So what did you do?

SON. I decided I would go home and tell my father that I was not worthy to be called a son. Just let me be as one of the hired servants.

INTERVIEWER. Sir, on that special day, were you looking down the road?

FATHER. I'd never stopped looking. But I couldn't believe it at first. I thought my eyes were playing tricks on me. He had been gone so long. I ran and grabbed him and kissed him!

SON. He not only forgave me, but he even gave me a ring, the best robe, and shoes. It was good to be home where I belonged.

FATHER. We had a big celebration! My son was dead, but now he's alive. He was lost, but now he's found.

INTERVIEWER, *to audience.* Just as this father welcomed his son back with open arms, so does our heavenly Father. I leave you with Luke 15:24. "For this my son was dead, and is alive again; he was lost, and is found."

End

Interview with Simeon and Anna

Characters

Reporter
Simeon
Anna

REPORTER. Hello, I'm Sara Abraham with WWJD News, reporting from Jerusalem. Just about eight days ago there was a big commotion in the "Little Town of Bethlehem," just a few miles down the road. It's been reported that a baby was born in a stable just outside of town. All the inns were full, so the family took shelter in the stable. The baby was born during the "Silent Night," and was laid "Away in a Manger."

People 'round about reported all kinds of strange things going on throughout the night—angelic beings, a very bright star shining in the sky, shepherds leaving their flocks to find this baby. All this commotion because a baby was born? Babies are born every day, aren't they? What was so special about this baby? There is a rumor going 'round that this baby is the Son of God! We're here in the temple in Jerusalem to talk to two people who may be able to shed some light on this "Holy Night." (*Turns to Simeon.*) Sir, what is your name?

SIMEON. My name is Simeon.

REPORTER. And yours, ma'am?

ANNA. They call me Anna.

REPORTER. Simeon, do you actually believe that this child—

SIMEON, *interrupting*. His name is Jesus.

REPORTER. Do you believe this child, Jesus, is the Son of God?

SIMEON. I know he is.

REPORTER. How do you know?

SIMEON. I am an old man. I have been waiting for the holy one who would be the light to lighten the Gentiles and his people, Israel.

REPORTER. What makes you think this tiny baby could be all that?

SIMEON. It was revealed unto me by the Holy Ghost that I would not die until I had seen the Lord's Christ.

REPORTER. How long have you been waiting for this to happen?

SIMEON. All of my life.

REPORTER. I understand his parents brought him here to present him to the Lord. What did you do when they came into the temple?

SIMEON. I took the baby in my arms and blessed God for sending him; that my eyes had seen him, and I could die in peace.

REPORTER. What did his parents think about all this attention given to their son?

SIMEON. Mary, his mother, marveled at these things. I felt sad that at some time she will feel the pain of giving up her son. With the coming of the Christ child, everyone will have to decide whether to accept or reject him.

REPORTER, *to Anna.* Ma'am, do you understand what Simeon is saying?

ANNA. Oh, yes! I understand perfectly. I, too, have looked for redemption in Israel.

REPORTER. Did you know that this child would be so special?

ANNA. I am an eighty-four-year-old widow. I pray and fast night and day in the temple. I knew he was the holy one when I saw him.

REPORTER. Could you tell us where the family is now?

ANNA. They have returned to Nazareth. The hope of the world has been born. We waited for him, and he is here.

REPORTER. Thank you, Simeon and Anna. You've made me want to know more about this one called Jesus. The prophet Jeremiah wrote these words in Lamentations 3:25–26. "The Lord is good unto them that wait for him, to the soul that seeketh him. It is good that a man should both hope and quietly wait for the salvation of the Lord."

End

Three Witnesses

Characters

Narrator
Joel
Naaman
Asa

(Curtain opens. Asa, Joel, and Naaman are standing quietly on stage.)

NARRATOR. *to audience from stage right.* Asa, Joel, and Naaman were witnesses of the Crucifixion of Jesus. A few days later, they are discussing what has happened.

JOEL. Do you mean to tell me, Asa, that you actually believe that man who was crucified was the Son of God?

NAAMAN. How could he be? His father was Joseph the carpenter, and his mother was Mary. They were just *regular* people, as far as I could tell.

JOEL. Yeah, Asa, don't you think he might have just been trying to make a name for himself? He sounded to me like a rebel who got the people all worked up. But then his plan backfired.

ASA. What do you mean?

JOEL He set himself up as a king who had come to help us, but he wouldn't even defend himself when he was arrested.

ASA. The chief priests lied about him and turned the people against him.

NAAMAN. I guess he did a lot of good, Joel. They say he healed some sick people. And how about taking five loaves and two fishes and feeding five thousand and still having twelve baskets of food left over? How do you explain that?

JOEL. Well, there was some kind of trick to it. He was clever all right, but in the end, all those tricks didn't save him. He died on a cross.

ASA. Did you hear what he said when he was on the cross?

JOEL I heard him say something, but the crowd was so noisy I couldn't tell what it was.

NAAMAN. I think he was begging them to let him live.

ASA. No, Naaman, he wasn't begging to live. He was saying *forgive*. I heard him clearly. I can't get it out of my mind. He said, "Father, forgive them, for they know not what they do."

JOEL. Well, he didn't mean us. We didn't do anything. We were only standing there watching. We didn't put him on the cross.

ASA. Maybe not. But we yelled with all the others to crucify him. I might have even yelled louder than anyone else. But now I feel differently. I am ashamed.

NAAMAN. He would have been all right if he hadn't called himself the "Son of God."

ASA. I believe he was the Son of God! Thinking back, he did lots of things that no one else could have done. You remember he brought that man back to life—and he had been dead four days!

NAAMAN. You mean Lazarus? I don't know. I always thought he was probably hiding somewhere those four days.

ASA. Tell me this, Joel. Why did it get so dark for so long on the day Jesus died? How can it be *that dark* in the daytime? And another thing, they say the veil in the temple was torn in two. Don't you think all that is very strange?

JOEL. I don't understand what made all these things happen. He had followers that might have had something to do with it.

ASA. I used to fish with two of his followers, James and John. They left their nets when Jesus came along. John was with him 'til the end. I saw him there at the cross with Mary.

NAAMAN. A lot of his followers are hiding, afraid of what's going to happen to them.

JOEL. Oh, with Jesus dead and buried, that'll probably be the end of the story.

ASA. Do you really think he's dead?

JOEL. Of course he's dead! He was crucified and buried in a tomb— end of story.

NAAMAN. I don't know. A friend of mine told me they can't find his body and that the stone was rolled away from the tomb. They found the clothes but not him.

JOEL. Well, I can explain that. The priests say his body was stolen by his followers.

Asa. They say he foretold that he would die and then rise on the third day. I don't understand it, but I've come to believe that it's true. I believe Jesus is who he said he was—the Christ, the Son of God. He was looking right at me when he said, "Forgive them." I'll never be the same.

Joel. Well, I don't believe it. I'll have to see him before I believe it.

Naaman. I don't know what to believe.

Narrator, *to audience.* As witnesses of the Crucifixion had a decision to make, we, too, have to decide. Who is this man called Jesus, and what do we do with him? Will you be like Asa, who opened his heart to let Jesus in? Will you be like Joel, who simply refused to believe and accept Jesus into his heart? Or will you be like Naaman, who just hasn't decided who Jesus is or if he wants him in his life? The choice is yours. Choose wisely.

End

Interview with Gideon

Characters

Reporter
Gideon

(*Reporter and Gideon are seated on stage.*)

REPORTER, *to audience.* Good morning. We're talking with that "mighty man of valor," Gideon, who led his army to conquer the Midianites. We've heard some talk about the battles, but we're here today to get the "rest of the story." Good morning, Gideon. Thank you for being here.

GIDEON. Good morning.

REPORTER. You have quite a reputation. Did you always want to be a military leader?

GIDEON. No, I hadn't really thought about it. I knew we needed one, though. The Midianites had oppressed the Israelites for seven years. We had to hide everything we grew in caves and dens to keep them from destroying it. I had always heard how God brought his people out of Egypt. But now, it seemed that God had forsaken us. But I was all wrong.

REPORTER. What do you mean? Wrong about what?

GIDEON. God had not forsaken us. We had forsaken him. God sent his messenger to tell me I had been chosen.

REPORTER. So you think God wanted you to be the next Moses?

GIDEON. I tried to get out of it. I told him that I was the youngest in my family and that I was okay just hiding out in caves from the dreaded enemy. I thought he probably knocked at the wrong cave door.

REPORTER. Apparently, he didn't accept that excuse.

GIDEON. No, God said, "I am sending you, and I will be with you." I never was so frightened. I couldn't believe what I was hearing.

REPORTER. How do you know it was God speaking to you? Maybe you just imagined it.

GIDEON. I didn't really know, and I wanted to be sure. Then the strangest thing happened. I told the messenger to wait there 'til I brought food out to him. When I brought it out, he touched it with his staff, and fire came out of the rock and consumed it.

REPORTER. Whoa! That must have told you something!

GIDEON. I knew then that he was an angel of the Lord, and I had seen him face-to-face. I thought I would surely die.

REPORTER. I would have. But you didn't.

GIDEON. No, I didn't. God had a plan, and God loves it when his plan comes together.

REPORTER. So now you knew for sure that you were going to deliver Israel out of the hands of the Midianites.

GIDEON. No, I wasn't ready yet. I knew only that God was able to send down fire to burn up a sacrifice. I was still scared. So I asked him for another sign of proof. I had to be sure.

REPORTER. What happened? What did you ask for?

GIDEON. I put a fleece of wool on the floor that night and said if there was dew on the fleece in the morning and not on the ground, then I would know that God would deliver Israel by my hand. And it happened! The fleece was so wet I wrung out enough water to fill a bowl.

REPORTER. And the ground was dry?

GIDEON. The ground was dry.

REPORTER. So that settled it, and you were sure.

GIDEON. No, I guess I'm very thick-headed. I still doubted, so I put the fleece on the floor that night, and this time I asked God to wet the ground but keep the fleece dry. And it happened! Just like I asked!

REPORTER. Well, you're right about one thing.

GIDEON. What's that?

REPORTER. You're thick-headed. I think I would have been convinced by now.

GIDEON. I then got my army together, all thirty-two thousand of them. But God said it was too many and for me to tell the ones who were afraid to go home. I felt like going with them. I was still afraid. Only ten thousand stayed.

REPORTER. Why shouldn't you keep the thirty-two thousand?

GIDEON. With such a large number my army would think their own hands delivered them and that God had nothing to do with it.

REPORTER. Now, you're ready to fight with the ten thousand?

GIDEON. No, God said that was still too many. So when we went to the water to drink, the three hundred who scooped up water in their hands were chosen to go with me to battle.

REPORTER. Three hundred out of thirty-two thousand?

GIDEON. Yes, and the enemy couldn't be numbered. There were so many of them.

REPORTER. How could you possibly beat so many with so few?

GIDEON. That's what I wondered. I wanted to trust God, but I was still afraid. But hearing the dream later made me know that God was with us.

REPORTER. What does a dream have to do with anything?

GIDEON. I overheard one of the enemy tell another that his dream meant that God was going to deliver Midian into my hand. If the enemy believed that God was on our side, why shouldn't I believe? Finally, I was sure, and I worshipped God.

REPORTER. You still just had three hundred men.

GIDEON. With God leading, three hundred would be enough.

REPORTER. Okay, now we get down to the actual battle. Tell me, how did you prepare your weapons?

GIDEON. That didn't take long. I divided the three hundred into three groups and told them to do as I did. Then I gave them their weapons.

REPORTER. Their swords and armor.

GIDEON. No, their trumpets, pitchers, and torches.

REPORTER. Come on. Be serious.

GIDEON. We were very serious. We surrounded the Midianites. At my command we blew the trumpets, broke the pitchers, and held up our torches. We shouted, "The sword of the Lord, and of Gideon." The enemy thought they were outnumbered. They were so confused they fought against each other, and we won the battle.

REPORTER. Well done! You will forever be known as the one who delivered the Israelites from the Midianites.

GIDEON. No, *God* delivered Israel.

REPORTER, *to audience.* So what should we do when we have battles to fight?

GIDEON, *to audience.* We pick up our trumpets, pitchers, and torches, and trust God to lead the way.

End

Where Is Your Treasure?

Characters

Narrator
Sam
Joe

(Curtain opens, Joe is sitting in chair gazing over audience. An empty chair is beside him.)

NARRATOR. *to audience from stage right.* Jesus had something to say to those who had many material possessions. Matthew 6:19–21 tells us, "Lay not up for yourselves treasures upon earth, where moth and rust doth corrupt, and where thieves break through and steal. But lay up for yourselves treasures in heaven, where neither moth nor rust doth corrupt, and where thieves do not break through nor steal: For where your treasure is, there will your heart be also."

SAM. *entering.* Hi, Joe. Nice day, ain't it?

JOE. Yeah, Sam, real nice. Come sit down for a spell. I'm just resting a bit, looking over my fields.

SAM. *sitting down.* Looks like your crops did well this year.

JOE. Yes, sir. Things have been better for me this year than they've ever been.

SAM. Why do ya think that is?

JOE. I know exactly why it is. *I* planted every seed just in the right place. *I* fertilized it perfectly, and *I* made sure it got watered real good. *I* did everything right.

SAM. What in the world are ya gonna do with all the fruit of your labor?

JOE. Ya know, I've been wondering about that myself. (*Stands and rubs his chin; then points yonder to the left.*) See those barns over there? I guess I'll tear them down and build bigger ones. And if they're not big enough, I'll build even bigger ones.

SAM. Well, that's one thing you could do. But I understand some of your neighbors didn't fare so well with their crops. They might have a hard time getting through the winter. Maybe you could help them out, since you're doing so well.

JOE, *ignoring Sam's remark, still looking yonder, rubbing chin.* Yes, sir, that's what I'll do. I'll tear down those old barns and build bigger ones. I'll have enough goods for years to come, and I'll eat, drink, and be merry.

SAM. You have it all planned out, don't you, Joe?

JOE. Yes, indeed. I've always had my life planned out. I figured first of all, I would learn my trade.

SAM. Then what?

JOE. Then I would set up my business.

SAM. Then?

JOE. Then I would make my fortune.

SAM. And then what?

JOE. What do you mean, then what? Just look around! I'm living good off the money I've made. I've done very well for myself. (*Rubs hands together.*)

SAM. What comes next?

JOE, *getting irritated.* Well, I guess someday I'll die.

SAM. And then what? Where will you be, and who will own all this?

JOE, *crossing his arms.* I'll think about that tomorrow. (*curtain closes.*)

NARRATOR, *reading Luke 12:20–21 from stage right.* "But God said unto him, Thou fool, this night thy soul shall be required of thee: then whose shall those things be which thou hast provided? So is he that layeth up treasure for himself, and is not rich toward God. Jesus also had something to say to those who did not have a lot of material possessions."

(*Curtain opens, Joe is sitting in chair. An empty chair is beside him.*)

(*Sam enters, and they begin their conversation anew.*)

SAM. Hi, Joe. Nice day, ain't it?

JOE. Really nice, Sam. Sit down for a spell. I'm just resting a bit, looking over my field.

SAM. Did your crops do well this year?

JOE. Not very well at all. Maybe too much rain, maybe not enough rain. (*Gets up and points to left.*) That field over there is about all we'll have to harvest.

SAM. You think that will get you through the winter?

JOE. Oh, yeah, that'll get us through the winter. We usually have enough to share with the neighbors. We've always had enough, no matter how much we had or how little we had. (*Pats stomach.*) You can see I'm not starvin'.

SAM. That's a good way to look at it. You never seem to worry about anything.

JOE. I've found out the Lord provides. Come here. (*Motions with hand for Sam to come closer to him.*) See those birds over there? They didn't plant any crops, and they don't have any barns to fill. God made 'em, and he feeds 'em. That's not sayin' they can be lazy—if they want to eat a worm, they have to pull it from the ground. So I figure if I trust God and do what I can do, God will take care of me.

SAM. That's good. And didn't he say something about the lilies of the field?

JOE. Yes, he did. He created the lilies. We didn't. King Solomon, in all his glory, could not compare to the beauty of the lilies. So I figure if God takes care and provides for the things that are here today and gone tomorrow, he'll take care of me.

SAM, *nodding head in agreement.* But I do have to say, Joe, it's too bad God didn't make you look as good as those lilies.

JOE. Yeah, well, that's all right 'cause he's still workin' on me—and on *you* too.

NARRATOR, *reading Matthew 6:33.* "But seek ye first the kingdom of God and his righteousness; and all these things shall be added unto you."

End

Back to "Normal"

Characters

Nathan
Levi
Narrator

(Curtain opens, Nathan and Levi stand still on stage.)

NARRATOR. *(Speaks from stage right.)* The place is Jerusalem, the day after the crucifixion of Jesus of Nazareth.

NATHAN. Maybe now, things will get back to normal.

LEVI. What do you mean, back to normal?

NATHAN. I mean like it was before.

LEVI. You mean before Jesus?

NATHAN. Yes, I mean before Jesus. Since he has been around here, everything has been turned upside down! I've not even been able to sell my goods in the marketplace this week because of all the commotion!

LEVI. The crowds *have* been terrible. People fighting each other, some *for* this Jesus and some *against* him. You couldn't even walk from one place to another without hearing something about him. I'm tired of it!

NATHAN. Well, things should get back to normal now—after what happened yesterday.

LEVI. Were you there? Did you see it?

NATHAN. No, I stayed home and tried not to think about it.

LEVI. I was there.

NATHAN. You were?

LEVI, *nodding head*. Not real close, but close enough to hear the sound of the hammer driving the nails. It still makes me shiver. (*Crosses his arms and closes his eyes.*)

NATHAN. It's a sad thing, that's for sure. But he brought it all on himself. (*Levi looks at Nathan questioningly.*) Well, if he hadn't been such a rebel, he'd be alive today.

LEVI. Maybe you're right. He sure got those religious leaders riled up.

NATHAN. I heard him call them hypocrites. He said they were like tombs—full of dead men's bones.

LEVI. What does that mean?

NATHAN. He said they were so busy trying to look good on the outside they forgot to clean up the inside.

LEVI. He did a lot of healing too, and that made them mad. I heard about the man who hadn't walked for thirty-eight years. Jesus told him to get up and walk. And he did.

NATHAN. Did you hear about him making the blind man see? He probably should have left him alone. After all, he had always been blind and was used to it.

LEVI. I think the blind man might have a different way of looking at that, don't you?

NATHAN. I guess so. But Jesus doing all these things on the Sabbath day was a no-no.

LEVI. I was there when he raised Lazarus from the dead. I couldn't believe what I was seeing. I don't know how he did that.

NATHAN. He said he was the Son of God. The chief priests didn't believe it, though. They said he was just Joseph's son, nothing more.

LEVI. He even talked about destroying the temple and building it again in three days. That really made 'em mad. If he had just kept still and gone about his own business, he would have been all right.

NATHAN. You know those men who followed him around everywhere? Only one followed him up the hill. The others deserted him when he was arrested. Who can blame 'em? Oh, well, like I say, maybe now things will get back to normal.

LEVI. Wait a minute. I just remembered. He told his followers he would be crucified, but he would rise again. What if that's true?

NATHAN. That's crazy! Why would he want to come back to a place like this? Look what they did to him.

LEVI. Yesterday was the strangest day of my life, so dark and sad. But it's over now. This is another day. He was here for a while. Now he's dead and gone, and in years to come no one will ever mention this man, Jesus.

NATHAN. Yeah, maybe now we can get back to normal.

(Both exit stage.)

NARRATOR, *reading Matthew 28:1–6 from stage right.*"In the end of the sabbath, as it began to dawn toward the first day of the week, came Mary Magdalene and the other Mary to see the sepulchre. And, behold, there was a great earthquake: for the angel of the Lord descended from heaven, and came and rolled back the stone from the door, and sat upon it. His countenance was like lightning, and his raiment white as snow: And for fear of him the keepers did shake, and became as dead men. And the angel answered and said unto the women, Fear not ye: for I know that ye seek Jesus, which was crucified. He is not here: for he is risen, as he said. Come, see the place where the Lord lay." (*Closes his Bible, pauses, and looks at the audience.*) Nathan and Levi will find out that since Jesus passed by, nothing will ever be the same again.

End

Peter on Trial

Characters

Judge
Prosecutor
Peter
Jury Foreman

(*Curtain is open, setting is courtroom.*)

JUDGE, *pounding gavel.* Order in the courtroom! (*Pounds again.*) Order, I say! We are here to decide the fate of Peter of Galilee. Order, I say! He is accused of keeping company with Gentiles. According to God's law, that is not permitted. Let the prosecutor begin.

PROSECUTOR. Peter, are you a Jew?

PETER. Yes, I am a Jew.

PROSECUTOR. Word has it that you've been associating with Gentiles. Is this true?

PETER. Well, if I may tell you—

PROSECUTOR, *interrupting.* You, a Jew, even ate with them. Right?

PETER. It all began one day when I was praying.

PROSECUTOR. Come on, Peter, get on with it. How do you plead? Did you or did you not break the law by consorting with Gentiles?

PETER. I cannot answer simply yes or no. Events have convinced me *that particular* law has been set aside.

PROSECUTOR. What? That's ridiculous!

JUDGE. Hold on. Let's hear what he has to say.

PETER. It was like this. I was staying at Simon's house in Joppa. I went upon the housetop to pray. I was very hungry, but before I could eat, I fell into a trance. In my vision, it was like heaven opened, and something like a great sheet was let down to earth. On the sheet was all kinds of animals.

PROSECUTOR, *with a look of disbelief.* A sheet full of animals. Yeah, right.

JUDGE, *showing interest.* What happened next?

PETER. I heard a voice tell me to get up, kill, and eat.

PROSECUTOR. And did you?

PETER. I said, "No, Lord, I have never eaten anything common or unclean." But the voice said whatever God has cleansed, don't call it common or unclean. It took a while to figure out what God was telling me. While I was thinking on it, something very strange happened.

PROSECUTOR, *in a mocking tone.* Stranger than a sheet of animals coming down from heaven?

JUDGE, *to prosecutor.* Shh! Continue, Peter.

PETER. Well, it seems that Cornelius, a Roman centurion in Caesarea, also had a vision at about the same hour that I had mine. In his vision, an angel had told him to send for me.

PROSECUTOR. Did you go? You knew this Cornelius was a Gentile.

PETER. The Spirit told me to go and not doubt. When I got there, I explained that it was unlawful for a Jew to keep company with a Gentile. But God had showed me through the sheet of animals not to call any man common or unclean.

PROSECUTOR. Why did Cornelius send for you?

PETER. He wanted me to tell him of Jesus and how he and his family could be saved.

PROSECUTOR. Surely you told him that Jesus came only to the Jews.

PETER. I told him what had been revealed to me—that Jesus came to save everyone. God is no respecter of persons.

PROSECUTOR. Can you verify these so-called visions?

JUDGE. Yes, Peter. What proof do you have of these visions?

PETER. The visions were verified by the Holy Ghost. As I was speaking to them of Jesus, the Holy Ghost fell on them as it did on us at the beginning. That's all the proof I need. Who am I to question what God does?

PROSECUTOR. *opening his mouth to speak, but then closing it.* I have no further questions, Your Honor.

JUDGE. Members of the jury, you have heard the testimony. What is your decision?

JURY FOREMAN, *standing up somewhere in the audience, unknown until now.* Your honor, we, the jury, find the defendant, Peter, guilty— guilty of obeying the Lord. And we want to do likewise.

JUDGE, *pounding gavel.* Court is adjourned!

End

Printed in the United States
By Bookmasters